AF753650

Building Enduring Client Loyalty

A Guide for Lawyers and Their Firms

Author
Susan Saltonstall Duncan

Managing director
Sian O'Neill

Building Enduring Client Loyalty: A Guide for Lawyers and Their Firms
is published by

Globe Law and Business Ltd
3 Mylor Close
Horsell
Woking
Surrey GU21 4DD
United Kingdom
Tel: +44 20 3745 4770
www.globelawandbusiness.com

Printed and bound in Great Britain by Ashford Colour Press Ltd

Building Enduring Client Loyalty: A Guide for Lawyers and Their Firms

ISBN 9781787424708
EPUB ISBN 9781787424715
Adobe PDF ISBN 9781787424722
Mobi ISBN 9781787424739

© 2021 Globe Law and Business Ltd except where otherwise indicated.

The right of Susan Saltonstall Duncan to be identified as author of this work has been asserted by her in accordance with sections 77 and 78 of the Copyright, Designs and Patents Act 1988.

All rights reserved. No part of this publication may be reproduced in any material form (including photocopying, storing in any medium by electronic means or transmitting) without the written permission of the copyright owner, except in accordance with the provisions of the Copyright, Designs and Patents Act 1988 or under terms of a licence issued by the Copyright Licensing Agency Ltd, 6–10 Kirby Street, London EC1N 8TS, United Kingdom (www.cla.co.uk, email: licence@cla.co.uk). Applications for the copyright owner's written permission to reproduce any part of this publication should be addressed to the publisher.

DISCLAIMER
This publication is intended as a general guide only. The information and opinions which it contains are not intended to be a comprehensive study, or to provide legal or financial advice, and should not be treated as a substitute for legal advice concerning particular situations. Legal advice should always be sought before taking any action based on the information provided. The publishers bear no responsibility for any errors or omissions contained herein.

Table of contents

Endorsements for *Building Enduring Client Loyalty: A Guide for Lawyers and Their Firms*

Susan Saltonstall Duncan has always been a leader in our industry, guiding law firms and other service providers to understand and deliver on a true value proposition. She has made a name for herself as a practical, thoughtful leader focused on ensuring that clients are 'delighted'. Susan has insight ranging across the legal landscape, grounded in real-life issues and actionable advice. *Building Enduring Client Loyalty* brings together Susan's counsel and leadership and, given the environment we are working in currently, her advice is even more relevant and needed. As clients search for their footing in the modern world and turn to their legal providers for far more, Susan's advice is timely and focused. She covers how to build a framework that ensures the right client focus but she also includes incredibly important advice on issues such as succession planning and onboarding new client relationships. Of particular note, Susan includes a 'healthy client roadmap' that lays out the core principles and practical steps to making us all more client-focused and driven to build client loyalty. I highly recommend *Building Enduring Client Loyalty* to legal service providers in all industries.
Lisa Damon, Partner, Seyfarth Shaw LLP

Building Enduring Client Loyalty reflects Susan's considerable knowledge and experience, keen insight and deep legal industry connections. It is an easy-to-read, concise yet thorough and practical tutorial on a most important and timely subject for law firm leaders to understand and drive within their law firms in order to succeed and grow in today's challenging and competitive legal marketplace.
David Foltyn, Chair and Chief Executive Officer, Honigman LLP

Susan Saltonstall Duncan is the undisputed master in capturing and articulating the keys to leadership in law firm/client relationship management. As someone who studied and coached firms on these issues long before others found it fashionable, she has both a long view and a wide lens on the law firm business model and what makes their client relationships successful. No one is better positioned to understand the realities of client loyalty and the relationship qualities that engender it (or diminish it). In this Special Report, readers will be privy to her treasure trove of strategic principles and practical tactics: I find her work in the areas of succession planning, 'distinguishing' value (in a marketplace full of excellent but fungible service providers) and life-cycle conversations about expectations and collaboration particularly valuable. Given ongoing disruptions to the law firm business model, rapidly changing client expectations and increasing competition from other providers (from the law department itself, to newly established law companies), how could a law firm leader (or future leader) overlook the opportunity to leverage Susan's wisdom?
Susan Hackett, CEO, Legal Executive Leadership LLC and former general counsel of the Association of Corporate Counsel (ACC – from 1989–2011)

Enduring client relationships are the key to success for all law firms. *Building Enduring Client Loyalty* is full of practical insights for creating and maintaining these relationships. Lawyers looking to build their practices would do well to read this book.
Tim Mohan, Chief Executive Partner, Chapman and Cutler LLP

This treatise by Susan Duncan, and her collaborators, is an exceptional in-depth and invaluable resource for general counsel, managing partners and their lieutenants in developing sustainable working relationships with their law firms, suppliers and clients. The timing of this publication could not have been better given the current environment. As *Building Enduring Client Loyalty* suggests, building strategic long-term relationships is the key to success. Everyone within the firm, including the senior partners and 'rainmakers', must put their self-interest aside and do what is in the best interest of their client and the firm. At DuPont, we emphasised the importance of investing in each other's success, which this publication does so well.
Thomas L Sager, former General Counsel DuPont and creator of the DuPont Legal Model

Building Enduring Client Loyalty distils a host of best practices and insights that teach us that client loyalty is less about what clients give to us than what we give to them.
Gary L Sasso, President and CEO, Carlton Fields

Acknowledgements

My sincere gratitude goes to the colleagues below, and to others who preferred not to be identified by name, for sharing their valuable time and insights with me. Given that the topic of this Special Report is client loyalty, I felt that it was essential to weave the 'voice of the client' into the content. We all have much to learn from their experience and perspectives as innovators and leaders in the profession.

- Lucy Endel Bassli, former assistant general counsel for legal operations, Microsoft; now founder and innovation coach, trainer and consultant, InnoLaw Group; author of *The Simple Guide to Legal Innovation* and online courseware *Modernizing Your Legal Practice*.
- Toby Brown, chief practice management officer, Perkins Coie.
- Amanda Bruno, chief business development officer, Morgan Lewis.
- Jeff Carr, former senior vice president and general counsel, Univar Solutions and FMC Technologies.
- Mark Chandler, executive vice president, chief legal officer and chief compliance officer, Cisco Systems, Inc.
- Kristen Cook, associate general counsel, 7-Eleven, Inc and SEI Fuel Services, Inc.
- Vincent Cordo, former central legal operations officer and global

sourcing officer, Shell Oil Co; now chief client development and relationship officer, Holland & Knight.
- Tom Flynn, general counsel and vice president corporate strategy, Budderfly.
- Heidi Gardner, distinguished fellow, Harvard Law School Center on the Legal Profession; faculty chair, Harvard Law School Accredited Leadership Program and Smart Collaboration Master Class.
- Maureen Harms, associate general counsel and managing counsel, 3M Co.
- Melissa Lauderdale-Ward, chief of staff to Thomas O'Neill, senior vice president and general counsel, Exelon.
- David Mack, senior vice president and chief legal officer, Hartford HealthCare.
- Christopher Marston, founder and CEO, Exemplar Companies.
- Catherine Moynihan, associate vice president, legal management services, Association of Corporate Counsel.
- Larry Richard, founder, LawyerBrain.

Part 1. Introduction

Many lawyers today still aspire to be a trusted adviser to clients and enjoy long-term relationships with them. However, building and maintaining loyalty has become much more difficult. For a decade or more, all sectors of the economy and society have experienced rapid transformations in relation to automation; technological capabilities; artificial intelligence (AI); blockchain and big data; globalisation and trade wars; medicine and telehealth; privacy and cybersecurity; talent engagement and competition; climate change; political unrest; and regulatory and compliance risk. The world seems to be in constant flux, presenting both threats and opportunities to businesses, families, communities, institutions and our way of life itself.

The business environment has been rocked further by the COVID-19 pandemic, which has caused disruption and volatility due to short and long-term effects that have upended the economy, social and business norms and activities through forced quarantines and medical crises. Law firms have been seriously tested through all of this turmoil. Many firms have proved agile and adaptive, but ultimately have not fundamentally changed their approach to client problem solving, service delivery or business models. The question now is whether and how relationships will be maintained, and whether loyalty between a client and a law firm will still exist in the 'next normal' environment.

I think there is a tremendous opportunity now for firms to build client loyalty. When clients are in pain – whether related to economic impacts, diversity and racial inequities, H1B visas or whatever they are struggling with – their lawyers can help them. Lawyers need to call their clients and offer to help. Clients still value relationships a lot. They like doing business with lawyers they like and who have saved their bacon in the past. Unfortunately, many lawyers and law firms are missing this opportunity to deepen loyalty, as they still are reacting and not proactively reaching out.

Toby Brown
Chief practice management officer, Perkins Coie

Client loyalty is increasingly difficult to define, earn and sustain. Heightened focus by clients on value; on efficient, cost-effective and innovative service delivery; and on doing more in-house and through automation has made it more difficult for law firms to maintain their positions. Firms are seeing increasing numbers of requests for proposals (RFPs) and increased competition from law companies, technology providers and clients themselves. Clients now employ procurement and legal operations professionals, who many law firms see as a threat to their relationships with in-house lawyers, because they oversee the law firm selection process and the pricing of fees.

Until a decade or so ago, law was primarily a relationship business, in which clients hired lawyers with expertise and experience in specific areas as needed. They retained advisers who they liked, often had friendships with and who treated them with respect. Today, clients still want to be loyal to their outside lawyers; but lawyers often make this difficult by ignoring client needs and the increasing pressures and changing environments in which clients operate.

This Special Report explores the full spectrum of relationship and service components that contribute to client trust and loyalty. Many clients – especially those with large in-house legal teams – have tightened their standards and expectations of law firms in terms of efficiency, cost-effectiveness, value-based pricing attached to outcomes and how services are staffed and delivered. Relationships still matter; but the personal aspects of relationships must now be accompanied by value pricing and value delivery. We hope that each of the chapters and topics, checklists and market insights in this Special Report will help lawyers and their firms to hone their relationship and delivery approaches to deepen their relationships with clients and earn their enduring loyalty.

Part 2. The loyal client framework

I. 'LOYALTY' AS DEFINED BY CLIENTS

The word 'loyalty' and the concept of loyalty mean very different things to different people. Some believe that 'loyalty' is a term better used to describe personal relationships, whereas 'trust' and 'stickiness' are more appropriate words in the business context. Because this Special Report explores how firms can build loyalty with their clients, we begin with the views of clients on how firms can both earn and erode their loyalty.

1. Lucy Endel Bassli

Former assistant general counsel for legal operations at Microsoft; founder and innovation coach, trainer and consultant at InnoLaw Group

I define 'loyalty' as having a deep level of trust with another person, for whom you are willing to stick out your neck. You go through ups and downs together and enable each other to succeed; you both have skin in the game and are willing to work on issues together. There is no loyalty between a company and a law firm; it all comes down to relationships between individuals, and sometimes those relationships go beyond those two people creating a sense of entity loyalty (the hardest kind to maintain).

History, longevity and deep relationships still are very important. One firm has been representing us for over 100 years and it still does cutting-edge work for us in labour and employment and regulatory work. We turn to this firm often for major litigation, and several of its lawyers serve as trusted advisers to a number of our executives and senior lawyers. They are on our panel because they were willing and able to negotiate rates enough, and they also share our values on diversity.

Head of legal operations, Fortune 100 company

Loyalty is still very personal, but is supported with substance. I will default first to my personal relationships with an outside lawyer. I give them a chance first and might guide them towards how to deliver work more efficiently to help them win the engagement. But there is a tipping point where I say, "I love you, I appreciate you, but if you don't change, I cannot keep sending you work." Relationships do matter; but now they must be accompanied by evident quality legal work and objectively defined successful outcomes.

2. Jeff Carr
Former senior vice president and general counsel of Univar Solutions and FMC Technologies

The differentiator for me, and why I am loyal to a firm, is culture. This is reflected in the chemistry, relationships, commonalities and connections I have with legal service providers – whether lawyers or other professionals. There has to be a cultural affinity and alignment with my providers, where their principles and mine mesh. One of my most loyal relationships I have had with an outside lawyer is with someone who says, "I wake up every day thinking about how I can get your company out of litigation and help it stay out of litigation." He understood better than anyone I had ever come across that we didn't want to be in litigation.

3. Mark Chandler
Executive vice president, chief legal officer and chief compliance officer, Cisco Systems, Inc

The 'loyalty' construct doesn't really resonate with me as motivation to make me want to work with a law firm and continue working with a law firm. Some factors that do drive 'stickiness' with my law firms include the following:

- Are they willing to say when they can't do the work?
- Do they have an appreciation of the business context I'm in? Do they understand the business decisions I am making, so they aren't just answering a legal question – they are answering a business question? I've described my job as "giving common-sense business advice informed by a knowledge of legal principles". I use law firms to make sure I get the black letter of the law right, if I'm not sure or confused about it. The great law firms will take it one step further and help me answer the business question.
- Am I getting value for money and how do I know? Are they willing to work on a basis that is tied to my success – not that they bear my business risk, but that they put their money where their mouth is in terms of outcomes? This is particularly true in

> the litigation space. How much of your fee are you willing to take on outcome? I've moved almost everything of significance to a fixed fee. Mine is a big enough company in volume that if one deal doesn't work out, the next one will; and as long as they are making money, they're happy. It has to be fair and be a partnership. That really builds loyalty, because then I don't have to think about the money. I don't then go out for bids on everything I have, because I know this is a team I like, I know they are competent and I know I'm getting value for my money; and I don't think I'm going to get a better deal from someone else.

4. Vincent Cordo
Former central legal operations officer and global sourcing officer, Shell Oil Co; now chief client development and relationship officer, Holland & Knight

There are three primary factors to loyalty. The first is the lawyer-to-lawyer relationships at all levels: top management connections are great, but don't forget about the team under the leadership that needs to know you and your firm. They are the ones asking which firms are to be invited to bid on work. Institutionalising relationships is important; rigour on getting to know others in the business is not optional. Contacts get promotions and shift roles, move on to other companies or retire.

The second is quality and economics: it is not about saving a per cent; it is results first. If the client received great value in the services delivered and good value for its spend, the firm stands to build on the portfolio.

The third is value services and the supporting cast: support professionals who make up operations – innovation, billing, pricing teams, for example – who work to help things run smoothly. Much work happens behind the scenes and involves asking the tough questions, monitoring the metrics and challenging the status quo – including ensuring the legal teams diversify which panel firms get invited to bid and then get selected so that legal spend remains with panel firms.

5. Tom Flynn
General counsel and vice president corporate strategy, Budderfly

At my prior company, we went through some pretty tough issues. We had offices in 10 countries and needed coverage in all of those markets. One lawyer at one firm really stood out and earned my loyalty. I defended that firm and continued to use it when the CEO and board encouraged me to use another firm that they thought was more credentialled and aggressive. The qualities that earned my trust included the following:

- He and his team really knew our business consistently; we never had to educate them about our company.
- He attended all board meetings at no cost to us.
- He took my many random calls and never nickel-and-dimed us by charging for many of them.
- He understood what I needed and made my life easier; he always had my back.
- He treated me like a colleague and peer, and was never patronising.
- He attracted good people to work on his team: the associate team was intact throughout the relationship and the communications and advice were coherent and consistent; everything worked very smoothly.
- He knew how to interact with me – he was low key and our styles meshed.

On the flipside, I used a global law firm for a particular need that required expertise in multiple countries, so we used lawyers in the firm's six different offices. I had a terrible experience. There was no

"To increase and sustain long-term loyalty with their clients, law firms must be innovative and mutually aligned to help each client meet its commercial goals."

Maureen Harms, associate general counsel
and managing counsel, 3M Co

single point of contact; the partners and associates were not connected to each other, so there was no coordination or consistency; and the work product I got back was terrible. It was a mark-up of my policy with comments marked all over the document by six different lawyers, some even inconsistent with each other. No one took charge of synthesising comments into a single, finished document. I sent it back and told them I wasn't going to pay for it, and then went to a single firm in one country which itself engaged firms everywhere needed and gave me a single, helpful work product.

One lawyer I inherited when I started at this company has a relationship with the company CEO. He is more interested in taking my CEO golfing than understanding our legal needs. At other times, he focuses on trying to convince the board that he knows more about the business than the management team. There is a revolving door of associates at his firm who make repeat mistakes; the partners never remember the names or roles of our leadership team (and we are a small company!). What the lawyer doesn't realise is that the CEO is completely deferential to me on all matters that are legal and I will get rid of him as soon as I can.

6. Maureen Harms

Associate general counsel and managing counsel, 3M Co

To increase and sustain long-term loyalty with their clients, law firms must be innovative and mutually aligned to help each client meet its commercial goals. As in-house counsel, we serve as trusted advisers who deliver high-quality, growth-oriented legal and business advice to our leaders and business partners. We need our external partners to break from the traditional hourly based advice model and provide better risk-adjusted legal solutions. Our best firms serve us in the same way we serve our clients: providing high-value legal advice at the speed of business.

7. Melissa Lauderdale-Ward

Chief of staff to Thomas O'Neill, senior vice president and general counsel, Exelon

The kinds of things that erode my loyalty to a firm include when it is resistant to negotiating rates or unwilling to consider or devise creative approaches to being compensated for delivering value; continues to use lock-step rate increases every year; is slow to bill us; doesn't share our diversity values; or is stuck in the old model of doing things.

Traditionally, loyalty was to an individual lawyer and was based largely on a long-standing personal relationship. Now it is to an individual or team of individuals at a firm based on the value that is added, with less focus on the long-term personal relationships. Personal relationships between in-house and outside counsel naturally develop over the years of working together, often in stressful and complex situations; but at the end of the day, the in-house counsel's role is to do what is best for the company, notwithstanding personal affiliations.

Loyalty is different now than it used to be 10 or 20 years ago. We still have loyalty to our preferred firms; but that loyalty is based on value, efficiency, knowledge of our business and the use of predictable, alternative fees. We will continue to stay loyal to our law firms as long as it remains a symbiotic relationship where we are both receiving mutual benefit. At the end of the day, though, it has to work best for us.

Associate general counsel, large franchisor

8. David Mack

Senior vice president and chief legal officer, Hartford HealthCare

Loyalty does matter. But I tend to look at a few select firms first to see if they have experience and expertise directly relevant to the matter. The firms that I contact first share similar traits:

- They are attentive to our mission; they understand healthcare and that, whatever we do, the patient is always our top priority; and they realise that we often work with a high level of urgency.
- They work within our model. The legal department is the law firm's client. There are still firms that don't work well with in-house lawyers and attempt to go around the legal department. That is 'legacy' thinking and does not create loyalty.
- They can meet our rate structure. We are a charitable organisation, so fees and costs matter. We heavily negotiate rates, including on our high-volume work. Fortunately, the firms we work with are all aligned with us on all other fronts.

Loyalty still is often to an individual partner, rather than a firm as a whole. Even when I work with others in a firm, I tend to turn to the relationship partner with whom I engaged originally, because I know he or she is aligned with us and understands our urgency, our organisation and our needs. That individual will oversee work being done by others without charging us, just to make sure the work gets done right, the way we need it and when we need it.

There is no longer a single firm that does everything for us. This is tied to the evolution in healthcare, which now requires national coverage and additional expertise. We tend to hire the right lawyer who is best in class for the matter. I recently hired someone new who had specific expertise we needed, but not at a firm we had worked with. We spent a few minutes confirming the lawyer had the necessary expertise, which is usually obvious, and the remaining hour on our expectations and culture. This lawyer is doing an extraordinary job supporting me in the transaction.

What has eroded loyalty? I have tried to provide feedback to some firms we have worked with in an effort to improve certain aspects of the relationship. I would rather try to solve issues and turn things around when needed. But if they can't fix it (or don't want to), then we need to make a change. Some firms really don't know how to change and are stuck in their legacy approach to providing legal services. Examples include not following our billing guidelines; failing to produce with a sense of urgency; or just being impractical by putting up too many barriers to getting to a good result.

II. CLIENTS AS LOYALISTS

1. Introduction

The goal for any law firm is to have as many loyal clients as possible. Loyalists are clients that remain clients for many years and – more importantly – that send repeat and new work to the firm, and actively promote it to their colleagues. Their loyalty is reflected and can be measured in their behaviour. It is important to note that not all long-term clients are loyalists: some have remained clients out of inertia, the loyalty of a senior executive or the high cost of switching work to another law firm.

The next type of client is one that is neutral or merely satisfied. It may be satisfied – or even very satisfied – with the firm, but it remains open to using other firms in search of better price, value or special expertise. These clients often do not stay with the firm over a long period of time; and while they may pay their invoices without pushing back, they cannot be counted on past each transaction. Another type of neutral client that is not fully loyal to the firm is one that may be using the firm because it has to – either because the firm has so much institutional knowledge that switching to a new firm would create knowledge gaps and pose a risk, or because the legal department has been required to use a specific firm by a high-level executive who has a personal relationship or long history with the firm.

At the other end of the spectrum are defectors and detractors. Defectors are clients that either leave quietly over time, taking new matters to new firms, or just stop using the firm without notifying it. This is usually difficult to do if there are multiple open matters, as a new firm would have to ask for the release of those files to begin working with the company. Detractors are the most harmful to a firm. These are clients that have had a negative experience and that actively criticise or deride the firm to their colleagues. Unfortunately, unhappy and vocal detractors are likely to share their negative stories with a much larger number of peers than loyalists share good stories; and given the power of social media today, criticism can go viral in a matter of minutes.

Several decades ago, Frederick F Reichheld and W Earl Sasser, Jr presented their findings from some ground-breaking research: reducing the number of clients who defect each year, which can often be 15% to 20% of your client base, can increase profits by 5% to 85%.[1] Further, as observed by Heskett, Sasser and Schlesinger, "one terrorist with a negative lifetime revenue stream ... can neutralize the positive returns from more than five other customers ... This further underlines the importance of insuring that the number of terrorists is minimized".[2]

Long-term loyal clients are much more profitable to law firms than merely satisfied clients. According to Reichheld and Sasser, this is because they increasingly retain the firm for more services from year to year; they cost less to the firm, as it does not need to get up to speed with a new client every year and can become more efficient; they send many referrals of new clients to the firm; and finally – though perhaps not quite as true today – loyalists who feel that they are getting great service and value from their firms tend to be willing to pay a price premium or at least not request sizeable discounts, unless they are sending higher and higher volumes of work.[3]

2. Evaluate and rank your clients

It is critical that firms understand the levels of loyalty and disloyalty among the clients that they currently serve. By assessing levels of loyalty, firms can turn neutral or merely satisfied clients into highly loyal clients, and address either defectors or detractors sooner and more productively. It is important for firms to consider whether the clients they have that are not loyal are clients that they want to keep. Frequently, firms spend a lot of time and provide steep discounts to clients that ultimately don't stay loyal to the firm, and that create other service demands or just generally seem never to be satisfied.

Firms should undertake an exercise of assessing their clients for loyalty, based on criteria that might include the following.

2.1 'A' client qualities (loyalists)

This type of client is willing to pay reasonable rates/fees in a timely manner and provides satisfying work that is complex and/or high-volume and repetitive. Ideally, the client is in a growth, acquisition or transition mode, and has many ongoing legal needs across practice areas. This might be a status or stature client that bolsters the firm's credibility and brand. The working relationship is one of mutual respect, in which there is good chemistry and communication. A loyalist speaks highly of the firm and as a result generates many new clients and referrals.

2.2 'B' client qualities (neutrals or merely satisfied)

This type of client pays fees in a timely manner, makes few demands and generates ongoing revenue. There may not be much growth potential or there could be unproven growth potential (eg, an entrepreneur). This client may only use the firm for specific matters or practice area expertise, and may limit opportunities for the firm to try to work with it in other areas. With this type of client, a relationship has been established, but there is no strong loyalty.

2.3 'C' client qualities (defectors)

A defector client is one with which the firm experiences regular collection issues, late payments and challenges to bills. This type of

"By assessing levels of loyalty, firms can turn neutral or merely satisfied clients into highly loyal clients, and address either defectors or detractors sooner and more productively."

client regularly pressures the firm to cut fees or provide cheaper rates, consistently choosing the lowest-cost provider for every matter. This client usually uses multiple lawyers and firms and has no primary firm loyalty to any of them. It sends RFPs for every matter, in part to get free advice, then chooses the cheapest firm or incumbent. None of the firm's lawyers have a close personal relationship or chemistry with anyone at the client organisation.

2.4 'D' client qualities (saboteurs/detractors)

Finally, the most destructive type of client is very difficult to work with, never pays invoices on time or in full, and is unreasonably demanding without rewards. This type of client puts the lawyers' or firm's reputation at risk or otherwise exposes them to legal risks, and often lacks ethics or integrity. The client likely has had a bad experience with the firm, but has not been candid with the firm about the problem or whether anything could have been done to fix it, and actively criticises the firm to peers and others.

3. How to manage client loyalty

Once you have assessed where you think your clients sit on the loyalty spectrum, it is wise to put processes in place to measure client loyalty; to move neutral clients up the loyalty curve; to attend to those that never will be loyal, but still take a lot of your time; and to address as best you can the reasons why clients are unhappy and actively sharing their criticisms with others.

Increasing loyalty and client retention, however, also means more closely and continuously monitoring all client relationships. This must become a mind-set that firm leadership embeds in all lawyers and staff as a key firm value: to attract and retain the ideal clients, turn them into loyalists and stay vigilant in listening to and remedying client problems and dissatisfaction.

3.1 Measure client loyalty

One of the simplest methods to measure loyalty is the Net Promoter Score®, developed by Frederick F Reichheld while at Bain & Company.[4] To determine the score, clients are asked a single question: "On a scale of 0-10, how likely is it that you would recommend [name of law firm] to a friend or colleague?" Those who respond 0-6 are detractors, 7-8 are neutrals and 9-10 are loyalists. A firm's score is calculated by subtracting the detractor score from the loyalist score.

3.2 Make feedback easy to provide

Firms should make it easy for clients to provide feedback at any time in real time, not just once a year during a feedback interview. This

"Never take your best clients for granted. The landscape is too competitive to be complacent. Continuously look for ways to be helpful and valuable to clients, to ensure their personal and professional success and to deepen relationships with them."

means they know who to call and have the name of someone who is not the primary partner on their engagement, in case they are reluctant to complain to that individual. All lawyers and staff working with clients should be encouraged and given an easy forum to share observations and complaints that clients express.

3.3 Reward your loyalists

Never take your best clients for granted. The landscape is too competitive to be complacent. Continuously look for ways to be helpful and valuable to clients, to ensure their personal and professional success and to deepen relationships with them. Make it a priority to show appreciation to them for referrals to new clients and ensure that new business development efforts, time and money are being spent on 'ideal' clients.

3.4 Enhance the loyalty of neutrals

Once you have identified clients in the 7–8 range of Net Promoters or when using a fuller client feedback tool, determine whether this ranking is your doing or theirs; what is preventing them from being fully loyal; and whether and how you might change that. For example, it could be that some clients don't know how to work with you more effectively or efficiently: they may want you to become more responsive, more service oriented or better at communicating; or you may need to more effectively explain the legal process and pricing upfront, including steps and strategies, attendant costs and risks, so that clients know what to expect, to be sure that you and the client are on the same page. If you cannot move your neutrals upward, determine whether you want to continue doing work for these clients. Also determine whether you should curtail the marketing efforts that led to your retention of these clients in the first place.

3.5 Understand and address defectors and detractors

Find out which clients are quietly taking their work elsewhere and why. For those that have had a bad experience with the firm, try to prevent or at least minimise the damage done to the firm by having a neutral party in the firm reach out to do a 'dissatisfaction' interview, similar to an exit interview of a departing employee. While it may be that you are glad that you or the client chose to terminate the relationship because they were sapping you of energy, time and satisfaction, it is critical to try to have some impact on damage control, since their complaints or criticisms may drive away prospective clients and give you or your firm a negative image.

Law firms still have the wrong business model. As long as they price work and are paid according to the 'value by head' or hourly, they are not incentivised to change. This does not support the agile way companies operate today. Instead, projects feel drawn-out. They aren't completed in the most efficient way possible. Even when firms give us alternative fee arrangements, many continue to work the same way. In-house legal departments are measured by operational excellence, just like any other function within the company. If our outside counsel's business models don't keep up, we will be forced to seek new alternatives.

Associate general counsel, multinational company

III. THE COMPETITIVE LANDSCAPE AND HOW TO STAY DIFFERENTIATED

1. Introduction

It is well known that clients have become much more discerning about who they rely on to fulfil their legal service delivery needs. Many clients believe that as much as 80% to 85% of their legal work is 'commodity' or routine work that often does not require the sophistication and cost of a large, expensive law firm and could instead be adequately serviced by alternative providers and/or automation tools. In-house departments are now focused on how they can most cost-effectively and efficiently support their companies, business units and executives, while allowing the flexibility to scale up or down as needed.

The options that clients now consider for their legal needs include using their own in-house lawyers, multiple outside law firms, law firm subsidiaries or captive alternative staffing companies (legal process outsourcers (LPOs)), alternative legal service providers/law companies (ALSPs), technology companies, e-discovery companies and subject-matter experts or management consultants. Outside the United States, many companies rely on the large accounting firms, which house teams of thousands of lawyers who practise law around the world. In the United States, the Big Four are establishing legal process and operations capabilities that are being offered directly to clients. While it is unlikely that alternatives to traditional law firms will totally replace law firms in the near future, clients are actively seeking providers that can deliver service and value efficiently and cost effectively.

2. New law companies, firms and providers

New law companies continue to proliferate and expand. They most typically are tech enabled, utilise various levels of non-traditional lawyers and professionals, and focus on process. Some of the largest employ more than 2,000 lawyers, accountants, data analysts, forensics specialists and project managers. Since they are operationally companies rather than law firms, they have infrastructure in place to rapidly staff a project, provide technology support 24/7, provide training and analyse data metrics. Clients also find it helpful that they can not only hire these providers on a project-by-project basis, but also select them on the basis of a specific need or skillset required. As a result, some clients may be using four or more of these providers at any given time.

Most of the work to date performed by law companies has focused on the development and adoption of technology and automation tools to address high-volume areas. These most often include agreements and contracts, such as master service agreements, non-disclosure agreements, commercial sourcing, sponsorship and licensing. Others track multi-state or international compliance requirements in specific subject areas, such as employment, tax, privacy and trade.

Consulting firms – including those that provide investigations, compliance, forensics and data analysis, and data privacy and security services – are often hired independently by companies in areas that overlap legal services. While many law firms have healthy and collaborative relationships with these consultants and are hired by clients to work together on matters, these consulting firms are also aggressively pursuing work that they claim they can do without the active involvement of a law firm.

We have worked with law companies – we have used them for some contract review and due diligence. But it is more difficult to develop a relationship and alignment, and the work product is limited in scope.

David Mack, senior vice president and chief legal officer, Hartford HealthCare

3. The Big Four: integrated legal advice in multi-disciplinary teams
Because bar associations in the United States have succeeded in barring multi-disciplinary practices (MDPs) and investment in law firms – at least to date[5] – law firms have not had to compete as directly with the Big Four in the US market. But as all global and international law firms know, the Big Four pose substantial competition to law firms outside the United States. Having retrenched after the Sarbanes-Oxley fallout, they have now rebounded into some of the largest law firms in the world and employ thousands of lawyers in every conceivable specialty on a global level.

The Big Four position their legal arms as offering the unique benefit of practical and strategic commercial advice together with legal solutions across multiple jurisdictions. They take a multi-disciplinary approach and collaborate across service lines to combine law with industry expertise, data analytics and risk management. By bringing diverse skills and experiences to the table, they can look at legal problems very differently from the way that traditional lawyers do.

4. Law firm alternative offerings
Law firms are finding innovative ways to service clients using multi-disciplinary talent and tools, despite regulatory roadblocks. Proponents of law firm multi-disciplinary and ancillary businesses understand that client needs often extend beyond traditional legal services. Legal problems and strategies often intersect with business priorities, economic analysis, public policy, business valuation, compliance and many other areas where consulting and accounting firms or individual professionals provide expertise.

Many have formed subsidiaries which are consulting or service arms that are wholly owned by the law firm. Most often, subsidiaries have been founded, and are often still run, by a partner in the law firm who wears two hats. Clients served are most often law firm clients; but

The Big Four do extremely well and dominate many areas in the world of consulting, which comes with large budgets and teams needed to support efforts. When it comes to legal services, they really don't perceive in-house legal department spend as a big enough opportunity yet to offer the level of value services, discounting, zero transfer cost proposals, secondments or write-offs on rates that law firms do. They just can't or won't offer that yet; but this doesn't mean they aren't working on ways to creatively add it to their portfolio. That makes them a potential competitor of firms, but a larger competitor of alternative service providers.

Vincent Cordo
Former central legal operations officer and global sourcing officer, Shell Oil Co; now client development and relationship officer, Holland & Knight

several subsidiaries also serve independent clients, provided that they have passed through the law firm's conflicts system. Occasionally, a firm will call a wholly owned subsidiary an affiliate; but more often, this term refers to a joint venture relationship in which there is shared revenue and profit or some other financial and legal contractual relationship.

The range of services offered by subsidiaries is broad. A recent inventory reflects the following capabilities:

- public affairs, government relations and communications;
- management and regulatory consulting (energy, electronic payments, strategic advisory, economic, life sciences, healthcare, international trade, Lean Six Sigma/process improvement, professional services);
- title, escrow and real estate services;
- insurance and claims management;
- investment and wealth management;
- venture capital and innovation incubators;
- privacy and cybersecurity;
- technology and e-discovery;
- project finance;
- construction/project management;
- facilities/relocation management;
- digital media and design;
- regulatory compliance tools;
- training and tracking; and
- trial consulting.

Integrated MDPs are service offerings housed within firms that are provided by lawyers as well as other professionals such as consultants, lobbyists, knowledge management and technology specialists, economists and practice managers. This is an approach to client problem solving in which multiple areas of expertise and experience are brought to the table. A fourth category of alternative service solutions applies to new tools and resources, many of which incorporate technology and process improvement tools to enable more effective and efficient service delivery models and information.

Most lawyers do not have the business experience or background and mind-set to think across all business disciplines, which is why bringing in other experts with different perspectives and technical knowledge is beneficial to clients. Lawyers who work together with others in an MDP can more effectively give clients the choice of working with a cross-section of experts to address their multi-disciplinary needs. This is what the Big Four are already offering and successfully doing outside the United States (now soon to be in the United States; see note 5), making them a most formidable competitor for non-routine legal services (these needs are often being met by other non-law firm legal service providers and LPOs).

5. Compete or collaborate?

Many of the new, tech-enabled law companies offer something that most firms have not invested in themselves; nor would many be well suited to do so. This is an area where client relationship partners should be initiating conversations – both with clients and with independent providers – to facilitate collaborative partnerships. The new law companies will continue to proliferate and clients will continue to need what they offer. The lawyers who embrace this and can work effectively in partnership will earn the support of clients in the future.

Clients are looking for value and for ways to achieve their needs more quickly, efficiently and cost effectively. The new law companies are addressing this by offering contract workers, but more frequently by offering a combination of technology and cheaper labour to execute more routine legal matters such as contract management, litigation discovery, some deal due diligence and compliance monitoring. Several law firms have developed their own subsidiaries to do this; others have

"Most lawyers do not have the business experience or background and mind-set to think across all business disciplines, which is why bringing in other experts with different perspectives and technical knowledge is beneficial to clients."

established relationships with these providers to be able to offer the best blended service package that will obtain the best results at the best price. Lawyers who want to be highly valued by clients will proactively approach clients to explore and propose this collaborative solution.

Many law firms have had a head start in building their own knowledge management platforms; AI-enabled processes using IBM Ross, Neota Logic and other platforms; e-discovery centres; project management tools; and service centres of contract lawyers, legal technologists and analysts in low-cost markets.

6. Differentiation: positioning and your value proposition

Even after you have been selected and engaged, clients may have buyer's remorse and worry about whether they have made the right choice. Right from the outset, you should make it clear that you intend to provide superior service and value, and that you want the client to keep you apprised of whether that promise is being delivered on.

It is likely that your new client is using many other firms, not just yours. You may have been selected for the new engagement because you have expertise that its other firms lacked; because your firm has more depth and scope and the ability to scale; or because you have developed a relationship with the current decision maker, who is interested in giving you a chance. Regardless of why you have been selected, a signed engagement letter does not mean that you no longer need to regularly reassure the new client that it has made the right decision to hire you.

Given the competition noted above, firms must be both clear and honest about what it is they do better than their competitors, including other law firms, law companies and consultants. One way to be sure that you are maintaining value and a differentiated brand is to seek regular feedback from clients and others to ensure that you are delivering on your differentiated promise. See Part 3, Chapter IV on how and when to seek feedback from clients and the marketplace.

IV. THE LOYAL CLIENT LIFE CYCLE

1. Introduction

Developing loyal and longstanding client relationships must be approached thoughtfully and systematically. There are a number of phases and steps in building a positive client relationship, from the firm's first interaction with the client – even before being retained – to its engagement and then throughout the relationship. The most critical consideration is that once a prospect becomes a client, lawyers and those serving it must continue and even elevate their selling efforts every day. The best firms and lawyers never take a client for granted or become complacent about nurturing the relationship to ensure satisfaction.

2. Win the work

2.1 Your credibility

This is the initial phase in which a prospective client has been referred to your firm. Ideally, the referral has come from a highly loyal client or another relationship; but other important influencers include your credibility and visibility as an expert in your service niche and perhaps the client's industry, as also reflected through thought leadership. Your

Figure 1. The loyal client life cycle

connections to regulators and other industry leaders could play a role; as well as your proven track record of staying ahead of the curve on issues and trends. Finally, whether you are on a client-approved provider panel, how you structure your staffing and pricing, and how effectively you are using technology to automate and increase efficiency will all impact on a prospect's decision to hire you (or to hire you again).

2.2 Your approach to selling

Focus first on helping prospects by being a resource, providing information and developing a relationship. Conduct research on the person, the industry and the company; ask good questions and listen intently. Assess the prospect's needs, gather intelligence and make yourself relevant and valued, so that you are among the first the prospect calls for insight and advice, even before being a client.

3. Deliver services/satisfy the client

3.1 Project management

The first engagement with a new client is a critical time to reassure them that they have made the right choice in selecting your law firm. Extra time 'off the clock' should be spent internally and with the client to conduct proper project scoping and project set-up, including establishing roles and responsibilities and setting and managing client expectations. The firm must be vigilant about producing quality work product and achieving milestones along a deliverable timeline. Budgets should be tracked and managed in real time, and the team should be communicating and collaborating.

3.2 The relationship

Every client has a preference for how to work with lawyers, including regarding interpersonal interactions. Many law firms encourage their lawyers to engage in personal style and communications style assessments, to help them better understand the motivations and styles of their clients (see Part 3, Chapter II for sample personality styles and behaviours). Some clients will forge close professional and personal relationships with lawyers; others prefer to maintain some distance. Building strong relationships with clients requires empathy, attentiveness and sustained effort and outreach.

4. Win a loyal client

4.1 Establishing trust

It is remarkable how many of the client interviews we conduct for law firms still reveal that many clients' top complaints about their firms or lawyers concern a lack of communication and responsiveness, or a high level of arrogance and 'deafness' to what the client needs or

"Many clients' top complaints about their firms or lawyers concern a lack of communication and responsiveness, or a high level of arrogance and 'deafness' to what the client needs or wants."

wants. It is usually smart to be transparent and clear, and to communicate early and often. Clients hate surprises and many want to be involved in determining legal options and strategy. In addition to reliability and responsiveness, clients want their lawyers to be accountable by doing what they say they will do and ensuring that others on the team and in the firm do the same. This also means taking ownership for mistakes and problems.

4.2 Anticipate, satisfy, nurture

Firms must be committed to continuous learning and improvement in order to strengthen long-term bonds with clients. Seeking feedback consistently and formally to identify areas for improvement and then acting on that feedback is critical to forming a partnership of trust with clients. Regular communication with clients enables lawyers to hear what is most challenging to them and to proactively provide insights on how peers are tackling these challenges. Providing value above and beyond the matters that clients engage firms for is an important way of deepening loyalty.

V. CUSTOMER EXPERIENCE – GOING BEYOND EXCEPTIONAL SERVICE TO EARN LOYALTY[6]

1. Introduction

As noted in the previous chapter, clients form impressions of you and your firm from their initial awareness of the firm and contact with you. Once they become actual clients, providing exceptional and consistent client service is critical to your success as a trusted legal provider. To develop and retain longstanding, loyal clients, however, lawyers and their firms must deliver an exceptional client experience.

Client experience encompasses all touchpoints that your clients have and the impressions they form of your firm. Therefore, you need to remember that your clients begin forming impressions long before they formally engage your firm, and that those impressions are further shaped after the engagement concludes. The typical client experience goes through various phases, as illustrated in Figure 2.

Figure 2. Typical client experience phases

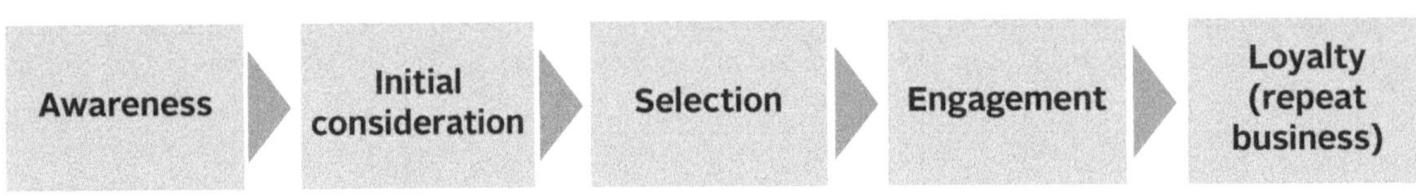

Even if each touchpoint of contact and service is theoretically good or even excellent, the client experience still may not be perceived as excellent because each of these represents only a phase in the overall experience. For this reason, the first step that a law firm must take is to map out the journeys that clients take over the life cycle of an engagement, and hopefully over a long-term relationship. In mapping these journeys, they must identify – through the eyes of their clients – where the critical junctures are for delighting clients and where the pain points in need of improvement are surfacing.

2. Client (customer) service versus client (customer) experience – is there a difference?

Customer service often focuses on the ways in which clients' needs are met through the delivery of professional, helpful and effective service during client matters or engagements. Excellent customer service involves:

- exceeding client expectations;
- being responsive;
- getting things done on time and on budget;
- anticipating and meeting client needs;

- being helpful, flexible and approachable;
- providing expertise and getting results; and
- delivering value.

Customer experience takes excellent client service one step further. Using a customer service mapping process, you can assess every interaction that your client has with the firm, from receptionists to executive assistants, billing and collections managers, pricing and business development professionals, and those involved directly in their legal work – paralegals and lawyers. The customer experience map should include:

- the client's experience from the time they became aware of the firm;
- what influenced and persuaded them to consider your firm;
- how the firm presented solutions for the client's needs;
- what feedback was sought immediately after the engagement;
- the client's interactions with administrative functions such as billing, pricing and technology;
- how the client felt working with the firm on a day-to-day basis;
- what follow-up steps were taken after the first engagement to incorporate client feedback and suggestions;
- whether the client felt that the firm added value; and
- the impact that the client's experience with the firm had on the client rehiring the firm and/or recommending it to others.

Customer experience is more than the touch points and tangible interactions that clients have with your firm. It encompasses the intangible aspects that your services create over time:

- how your clients feel about your firm and your brand;
- how you make the client feel;
- what your firm stands for; and
- the promises you make and whether you deliver on them.

Law firm clients will evaluate their satisfaction and loyalty based on the overall customer experience – their cumulative experiences over multiple touchpoints over time.

Law firms too often focus primarily on their services and their technical expertise. Many are getting better at understanding and improving on how they deliver services; although many still fall short on being easy to do business with and on consistency across departments and offices, and even from lawyer to lawyer. Few firms focus on how helpful they are to clients; how all lawyers and personnel at the firm come across to clients; and how clients feel having worked with the firm. These latter characteristics are critical aspects of delivering an exceptional customer experience.

Client service is still very 'blah'. Clients and lawyers often find themselves in a loveless relationship, in which clients are unhappy about a lack of engagement, unresponsiveness and ineffective communication. The relationship is historical, likely based on predecessors, and the current responsible parties are afraid to make a change. Excellent customer experience doesn't really exist; but because legal substance is still top priority, clients continue to work with those lawyers despite a consistently poor service.

Lucy Endel Bassli
Former assistant general counsel for legal operations at Microsoft; now founder and innovation coach, trainer and consultant at InnoLaw Group

3. Client journey mapping
At its core, client journey mapping is a qualitative process that involves seeking out the client's perspective on the experience, typically via an in-person or phone interview. Who conducts these interviews can vary. While some firms may choose to engage third-party consultants to uncover insights and aggregate client experiences across various touchpoints, others may wish to leverage internal people – perhaps a chief administrative officer, chief human resources officer or chief marketing officer – to lead this process.

The important factor is that whoever is conducting the interviews:

- knows the right questions to ask;
- can remain independent regardless of internal connections, politics and loyalties; and
- can assimilate what he or she is hearing into a fair, accurate and discrete mapping exercise that lays out the different ways that clients experience the firm.

As with most research, client participants should be afforded anonymity. In other words, unless clients want their experiences attributed, their feedback should remain anonymous and aggregated with that of others, without any identification of who the feedback has come from or who it may have been directed to. Client journey mapping is about discovery, not a witch hunt.

I always remember the quote from Maya Angelou, "I've learned that people will forget what you said, people will forget what you did, but people will never forget how you made them feel." Clients want reassurance that you've got their back; that you can help them if they are overloaded and resource constrained. They will remember what you do, not just what you say.

Former chief of staff and senior director of legal operations, multinational technology company

Effective journey mapping requires that an organisation look at all of the touchpoints and operational aspects of generating awareness and engaging with and getting work done on behalf of a client. This is particularly difficult to do in law firms, as partners often have their own way of doing things, which may not follow a common path that is mandated by the firm. Partners often act independently of each other and don't always communicate effectively with other partners and lawyers on the team, to say nothing of paralegals, contract attorneys and legal support professionals. Then there are all the other client-facing and back-office support personnel with whom clients often interact: administrative assistants, receptionists, conference/meeting set-up attendants, billing and collections personnel, IT staff and e-discovery and legal research professionals. Furthermore, firms often operate in silos, which not only presents major challenges to service consistency, but also creates potential disconnects between all the critical touchpoints along the client journey.

4. Superior customer experience leads to greater loyalty and revenue
Superior service leads to high satisfaction, which leads to greater client loyalty. Having clients as 'loyalists' who consistently advocate on

"Having clients as 'loyalists' who consistently advocate on your behalf is the goal that every firm should have with every important client, especially since it leads to higher profitability."

your behalf is the goal that every firm should have with every important client, especially since it leads to higher profitability. Many renowned management consultants have researched and quantified that firms that deliver exceptional client service and consistently rank highly on Net Promoter Scores earn stronger client loyalty, which converts to clients that engage the firm for additional services, make recommendations to colleagues and substantially increase the lifetime revenue value.

5. Steps to implement a customer experience assessment process

- Get commitment and active involvement from top leadership to create a customer first/superior customer experience corporate attitude. This will require time and resources, and likely will result in changes to policies and normative behaviours within the firm and an openness to constructive criticism and continuous improvement.
- Establish a cross-functional leadership team to drive, monitor and support the initiative.
- Dissect and better understand the current customer service experience. This will include the following steps:
    - Institute formal and ongoing feedback mechanisms internally and externally to fully capture from clients' perspectives what you do, how you do it and how it makes them feel.

    - Map out the customer journey at every point of interaction and depict the journey from the client's perspective, not the firm's.
    - Determine which aspects of the journey are most important – that is, those which create the most impact overall (either negatively or positively). Where differences in customer experience exist, try to discern whether there is a connection to a practice group, client team or office.
    - Break down the silos; hold a series of brainstorming sessions of cross-functional teams together to develop improvements.
    - Provide certain tools, worksheets, templates, approaches, processes and timelines to support smaller teams as they further interpret and assess the customer journey and generate ideas for driving change into various facets of the business that will impact on the client experience.
- Build in expectations and empowerment of all employees to innovate on continuously improving the customer experience:
    - Build in customer experience attributes and actions to all lawyer and employee performance evaluations.
    - Devise metrics, measurement schedules and reports.
    - Institute formal and ongoing feedback, including internal surveys and focus groups, external client interviews, end-of-matter surveys, customer journey touchpoints/pain point assessments and Net Promoter Scores.
- Reinforce the vision and values by:
    - training and developing all employees;
    - measuring performance against expectations; and
    - recognising and rewarding those who innovate and deliver superior performance that ultimately delivers an end-to-end outstanding customer experience.

Part 3. A roadmap: getting started on the right foot with new clients

I. BUILDING THE FOUNDATION OF BEING TRUSTWORTHY AND TRUSTED

1. Introduction

Strong relationships are built on a foundation of trust. It does not matter in what context your relationships exist – whether personal, social, professional or civic, you will not build successful, mutually meaningful and beneficial relationships without being authentic and trustworthy. In the context of business development and client relationships in law firms, trustworthiness is essential to earning the right to represent clients, including expanding services to them when it becomes clear they need them. Since trust is about personal relationships and behaviour, it is developed by individual lawyers with individual client contacts. It is not 'institutional' – that is, the law firm itself cannot develop trust with a client contact.

In mid-sized and large law firms, the best service to clients and opportunities for growth often occur between and among the lawyers and other personnel in the firm. Lawyers overlook the importance of building trust with their internal colleagues, which ultimately impedes their ability to strengthen client loyalty and serve the broader needs that clients may have.

Lawyers and law firms that want to cultivate long-term, loyal client relationships can do so only if clients experience the lawyers and staff as trustworthy. Trust occurs through repeated interactions and increased intimacy, through which clients feel comfortable sharing their views, concerns and feelings, and fundamentally believe that the lawyer has their best interests at heart. There are several key characteristics of trustworthiness to attend to and improve upon to strengthen client bonds, as discussed below.

2. Credibility, competence and reputation
Lawyers demonstrate credibility through:

- technical legal knowledge;
- deep expertise in a niche or industry;
- the results they achieve in their cases and transactions;
- understanding of a client's business; and
- thought leadership.

Lawyers who are credible anticipate issues before they arise, look around the corner and plan ahead for the client. Competence is also often conveyed in executive presence and the self-assurance that lawyers project when speaking and interacting, without being

"Trust occurs through repeated interactions and increased intimacy, through which clients feel comfortable sharing their views, concerns and feelings, and fundamentally believe that the lawyer has their best interests at heart."

domineering or arrogant; as well as in their passion and enthusiasm for what they do as lawyers.

3. Integrity, honesty and openness
Trustworthiness is enhanced when lawyers are honest and transparent with clients. Lawyers who speak the truth and don't exaggerate or embellish are more believable. Clients also respect lawyers who admit when they don't know something or when the firm doesn't have the expertise for a particular need and provide a good referral to another firm. Lawyers need to 'take a point of view' and be willing to address the elephant in the room. If mistakes are made, trustworthy lawyers admit their mistakes (or those of the firm or team), and are willing to be held accountable rather be defensive or throw someone else under the bus. Finally, being trustworthy also means maintaining confidentiality so that clients feel safe sharing their concerns and frustrations, and ultimately open up to more risk and vulnerability.

4. Reliability and consistency
Being reliable means that others can trust that you'll do what you say when you say you will. This is demonstrated through actions, not words – for example:

- consistently delivering on your promises;
- meeting or beating deadlines;
- delivering on objectives and outcomes; and
- staying within budget.

Lawyers can convey reliability by:

- setting expectations with clients upfront and reporting regularly;
- being on time for meetings and phone calls;
- communicating frequently and proactively; and
- returning emails and phone calls within four to six hours, even if just to say they will respond in greater detail later.

Clients often complain that there is inconsistency of quality from lawyer to lawyer or office to office within the same firm. Lawyers should ensure that they:

- are consistent with information, service approaches, pricing and outcomes;
- are error free with work;
- set and follow agendas; and
- provide necessary information in advance of meetings, so that clients feel prepared.

5. Empathy, caring and helpfulness

Putting yourself in your clients' shoes is essential to demonstrate that you understand their issues and their personal agendas, and the internal politics, stakes and challenges that may be at play. Being caring and helpful means always putting client needs and goals before your own and offering to help them with issues not related to a particular matter, or even to work. Demonstrate empathy by listening carefully not only to words, but also to feelings. Clients will feel well cared for if they know that you have their back and are always thinking about them. Be helpful to clients by making them look good and by writing cover emails, summaries and even board presentation slides that they can easily forward to their executives or stakeholders. Developing this aspect of trustworthiness will also require you to open up about yourself, your personal interests and family, and perhaps your own vulnerabilities.

Unfortunately, lawyers have not always demonstrated or nurtured trustworthiness. Traditionally, it was common and acceptable for lawyers to convey that they were smarter than others – especially 'non-lawyers' and even in-house lawyers. In client meetings and pitches, they often conducted monologues instead of dialogues, coming across as condescending, arrogant and self-centred. To ensure that you are being client or other-centred, check yourself to be sure that you avoid:

- interrupting others;
- dominating conversations;
- rushing to a solution by assuming that you know what is right without listening fully to the client;
- being distracted during meetings by checking emails or reviewing non-client documents (or taking a phone call);
- overselling/embellishing credentials or bragging;
- putting your agenda and best interests first, ahead of the client;
- always having to be right; and
- looking uninterested, bored or unengaged when interacting in meetings or calls.

II. UNDERSTANDING CLIENTS

1. The organisational client: the business, industry, cultures and values

Traditionally, lawyers have been excellent legal technicians, but have not always been good at positioning the legal issues that they have been asked to address within the broader context of a client's objectives and organisational business strategy. Clients want their lawyers to understand their industries and the challenges they present.

In the corporate world in particular, clients often criticise their lawyers for not being 'commercial' enough or customising advice to their specific company needs. 'Commerciality' means understanding legal issues and approaches in the context of the business's goals, risk profile, risk tolerance and budget. Clients want their lawyers to do more than read their financial statements; they want their legal advisers to know about their business strategy and business plan.

Clients today face far riskier business environments than they did even a few years ago. They want and need advisers who can assess current risk, but who can also counsel them proactively on risk triggers and solutions, as well as peer benchmarks. Only a certain amount of commercial knowledge can be gained from business plans, the company's website, financial statements, industry sector websites and other online sources. The best way to be truly commercial on behalf of clients is to talk regularly to them about their issues, industries, priorities and personal agendas.

The areas to explore at a company/organisational level include:

- how recent events affected the client in the last fiscal year;
- what changes the client has made or plans to make in light of those trends or events;
- what the company's financial position, health and philosophy are;
- the business plan and strategy for the next three years, the challenges that are anticipated in trying to meet those goals, and whether acquisitions or divestitures are part of the strategy;
- new products, services or offerings that the client is developing;
- specific opportunities and threats facing the business and the client's industry;
- how the client is organised (in functional or business units, hierarchal or flat);
- the organisational chart, to reflect the legal department's structure and other functional areas;
- the client's values, cultural norms, and philanthropic and corporate social responsibility philosophy;

- how the client operates – in silos or collaboratively across units/functions;
- how and by whom key decisions are made and executed;
- the industries and markets that the client is in, now and in the future;
- the client's customers, competitors and distribution channels;
- the client's technology and data environment, privacy and security risks;
- the client's labour and employment culture, policies and climate; and
- the client's current and projected legal needs, annual budget and service providers.

2. Individual clients: roles, career aspirations and personal lives
Clients are not a single entity – they are comprised of individuals who have different perspectives, backgrounds and preferences. Building rapport and trust requires that lawyers get to know their clients as people. On the professional side, this includes:

- what drives and motivates them;
- what their career aspirations are;
- what they like and don't like about their role or their company;
- what the political climate is for them inside the company; and
- what their personal stumbling blocks are.

As noted later in this chapter, it also includes understanding:

- their personal styles and tendencies for working and communicating;
- their tolerance for risk; and
- the resources that they access (ie, peer networks, professional advisers, industry and professional associations).

On the personal side, the goal should be to get to know clients and try to find areas of commonality that you or someone else in your firm has with the client. Rapport-building questions and discussions can focus on home towns, college, graduate school, career paths and prior work experience, families, hobbies, favourite holiday spots and interests such as travelling, biking, hiking, golf, skiing, sports, cooking, gardening, wine and civic or charitable activities or passions.

In addition to getting to know clients at an individual, personal level, it is critical that lawyers understand the pressures that many of them face. Clients often bemoan the fact that their outside lawyers seem oblivious to the pressures they are facing in their legal departments and in the companies themselves. For example, most general counsel now serve a critical role in the business as a part of the executive team, counselling CEOs on risk and compliance and strategic issues. Additionally, the annual compensation of many general counsel is often tied to how well the legal department does, especially in terms of achieving cost-cutting and efficiency goals. One of the most valuable things that a law firm can do is to spend a day off the clock at the client's office facility to meet others, walk the floors and see how the business operates.

3. Understanding different communication styles and personalities

Clients develop deeper relationships and long-term loyalty with lawyers they know, like and trust. No two clients are the same, however – not only in the roles they may have in their companies or in their experience and background, but also in how they see the world. In order to build stronger relationships with clients, lawyers must have clear self-awareness and an understanding of what motivates their clients, as well as the looking glass through which their clients hear and respond to things.

Lawyers who have truly loyal relationships understand their own tendencies, know how they react to people and circumstances, and can understand and adapt their behaviour to others' styles. There are

"Clients often bemoan the fact that their outside lawyers seem oblivious to the pressures they are facing in their legal departments and in the companies themselves."

a number of well-known psychometric assessments used in the workplace today, including DiSC®, the Myers-Briggs Type Indicator®, Strengths Finder and the Hermann Whole Brain® Thinking Tools. One of the newest on the market is a tool called Smart Collaboration Accelerator®, which evaluates seven behavioural traits associated with collaboration – a quality that clients increasingly value. Each is different in its diagnostic focus on behavioural tendencies, personality, communications, motivation and values, and leadership styles.

In order to deepen client relationships, it is important for lawyers to understand their own style, preferences and tendencies, to see how others may perceive and react to them, and to help coach team members on how to more effectively interact with them. It is equally important for lawyers to understand their clients' styles and preferences, in order to adapt their approaches and communication styles to each client. Even without the benefit of knowing for certain a client's psychometric profile, it is relatively easy to make some assumptions and then tailor your approaches accordingly. Try to use the following guidelines to interpret your client's style and consider some approaches that you might take to better communicate and interact. Be aware that while most people have a primary and secondary style, no one is limited to the traits in one type only.

"Lawyers who have truly loyal relationships understand their own tendencies, know how they react to people and circumstances, and can understand and adapt their behaviour to others' styles."

3.1 Type 1: Relationship-oriented, cautious

These people tend to build close, loyal and longstanding relationships with family, friends and colleagues. They are driven more by the emotional/feeling side of the brain than the fact-driven, analytical side. They are caring and are often very involved in civic and community groups. Harmony is really important to them and they are very uncomfortable with conflict, so they tend to be indecisive and avoid taking chances. In order to keep the peace, they are often more agreeable, accommodating and cooperative. They socialise often and need to be accepted by others. They are very risk averse and nervous about being wrong, about change or about trying something new, so may be slow to make a choice or decision.

If your client reflects these tendencies, remember that you must develop a warm, genuine relationship before they will trust you. They gravitate towards people who care about them as people and don't want to be hurried in conversations or decisions. With these clients, allow plenty of time for small talk. They prefer simpler explanations and a conversational style. Stay away from suggesting risky options or uncertain results, as they need to feel secure.

3.2 Type 2: Analytical, cautious

These types of people can be perfectionists who are very interested in detail, precedence, proof, facts and data, and hate to be wrong or criticised for their work. They tend to be well disciplined and exacting, prefer being in control and are risk averse. They offer stability to their companies, but are often harder to get to know, as they are cautious about developing relationships and can be perceived as uncaring or aloof.

If your client has these tendencies, communicate with them through facts, numbers, diagrams, charts and prior cases or deals. They want to know what their peers are doing before choosing an approach or solution, and will take time to analyse their options before making a decision. They don't like to be rushed; and if you try to do so, they may withdraw.

3.3 Type 3: Results-oriented, dominant

This type of person likes to make decisions and get things done quickly. They typically do not like to engage in a lot of small talk because they hate to waste time, and are not as social or as interested in developing deep relationships. They are competitive, assertive and can be confrontational. They tend to speak quickly and dominate conversations. Type 3 people want to be in charge and make their own decisions, and may appear uncaring, as their first priority is to get things done – sometimes seeming to be unconcerned for the people involved.

If your client is this type of person, you should avoid too much small talk and get right to the point. These clients want direct and honest assessments in succinct, bulleted formats where you tell them their options and probabilities of success, but you do not tell them what to do, as they want to be in charge and make their own decisions.

3.4 Type 4: Big-picture thinkers, expressive

This fourth profile reflects people who like interacting with people, are enthusiastic and excitable and talk a lot, often dominating conversations. They tend to have many social and professional relationships (they probably have thousands of LinkedIn contacts!), although most of those will not be deep. They are often 'dreamers', focused on the big picture, and think creatively, intuitively and optimistically; they like variety, but may be less disciplined about getting down to the minutiae of execution. They like and even seek out personal recognition and are willing to take chances on hunches.

Clients that display these tendencies will appreciate you taking time to develop rapport and to spend time socialising with them. Since people are important to them, they will want to know and meet people on your team. These clients will want to explore different options with you and may take more time than they need to do so, and will not want to engage in disagreements or controversies. They want to think big and dream about possibilities, but may not be adept at converting ideas into execution – so be sure to provide them with plans and timelines to keep them on track. If you have an opportunity to nominate this client for an award or recognition, co-author an article with them, place them on a panel or invite them to lunch at a popular restaurant or club, they would enjoy and appreciate this.

III. ONBOARDING NEW CLIENTS – ESTABLISHING MUTUAL EXPECTATIONS AND PROTOCOLS

1. Introduction

The customer service experience begins long before a client actually engages a firm. In some cases, the process of actually opening a new client file may create some stressful interactions over things such as conflicts and conflict waivers, staffing and billing requirements and other new engagement protocols. Because first impressions as a paying client (as opposed to a prospect) will have a disproportionate impact on the client's perceptions, it is critical that their experience as a new client goes smoothly and comfortably.

Every firm should utilise an onboarding checklist of standard steps and conversations to undertake with each new client. Many clients already have their own guidelines and protocols (see Appendices I and II for two examples). A client's experience with a firm should be consistent across lawyers, practice groups and offices; not individualised depending on the relevant lawyer's new engagement approach. Some firms have developed client 'pledges' or 'promises' that articulate publicly what the firm's commitment is to clients and how it expects its lawyers and employees to proceed in order to fulfil these

"Some firms have developed client 'pledges' or 'promises' that articulate publicly what the firm's commitment is to clients and how it expects its lawyers and employees to proceed in order to fulfil these standards."

standards. Lawyers and employees are measured on their performance against the client service standards.

At the outset of every new client relationship and at least annually thereafter, it is recommended that firms take the following steps.

2. Establish an internal central knowledge base

It is very likely that during an RFP stage, a client convergence process or a less formal prospecting effort, the firm will have collected competitive intelligence and business and financial intelligence, and captured its history and relationships with the client. This should all be held digitally in a central repository and made available to anyone internally who will be serving that client.

It is important to have an organisational chart that reflects all key personnel in departments and subsidiaries, and the chain of command and levels of authority and decision making. If the firm is inheriting a client partway through a major dispute or transaction, or even if shortly thereafter, prior legal documents should be catalogued. Other important information to gather includes:

- corporate structure;
- capital structure and financing documents;
- employee manuals;
- policy documents and training manuals;
- privacy and cybersecurity protocols; and
- regulatory risk profiles.

3. Develop a written service plan with the client

Assuming that the client does not have its own, this document is created together with input from the client and will clarify the client's objectives, their philosophy about their legal strategy, criteria for successful outcomes (or at least how criteria will be determined for each matter) and general preferences for working with their outside law firms. Also described are the methods and frequency with which the law firm will request feedback from the client for continuous improvement. The client's billing, staffing and reporting requirements can be included in this document. Once finalised, this service plan should become part of the client repository described above, so that all new team members can review and follow the guidelines.

4. Communicate effectively and avoid surprises

One area of continuing frustration for clients concerns communications and responsiveness. The client team or relationship partner should establish protocols that will meet the needs of clients, including:

- reporting relationships;
- how and to whom documents and drafts will be circulated;
- preferences in format (email, phone, text, paper mail);
- expected deadlines and response times; and
- relationship check-ins (how often and with whom).

Develop an organisational chart of internal and external team members, their emails, direct dials, mobile phone numbers and roles. Make this available to clients and internal team members. Never surprise clients with budget overages or inaccurate bills with errors or mistakes. Keep the client apprised of overages during a matter; call ahead if a bill exceeds budget and always ensure that the client knows who is working on a case. Let the client make decisions about strategy options based on outcomes and cost implications.

What erodes my loyalty is when firms don't communicate and don't do what they say they will do. We have had an experience with one firm where they agreed to a budget and blew through it seven times, but didn't tell us until three months afterward. This same firm keeps asking to meet with us because they tell us they want to improve. So we meet with them, provide feedback and they never follow up on what we tell them. In fact, they don't really communicate proactively with us at all. I am always the one chasing them down.

Associate general counsel, multinational company

5. Agree on service, staffing and billing protocols and standards

Clients often have their own billing protocols that they require law firms to follow. Everyone on the team must become familiar with these, and the firm's IT and billing professionals must ensure a quick set-up to ensure that the protocols are made compatible with the firm's timekeeping and billing technology. If clients do not have their own protocols, discuss the firm's processes, format, level of detail and timeline to ensure that these work for the client.

The client and firm should discuss how matters will be staffed and what internal resources the client will use or have access to, as well as whether it already has a relationship with a law company or e-discovery vendor. Discuss disbursement policies and the management of litigation expenses – for example, will the client put money into an escrow to cover expert witness costs and other items which often require an upfront investment? Clients often specify what they are or are not willing to pay for – for example:

- a first-year associate's time;
- having no more than a certain number of lawyers billing time for the same call or meeting; or
- transferring knowledge to a new member of the team.

Increasingly, clients are insisting on diverse attorneys to manage and get origination credit for their matters. Firms should be proactive in establishing diverse teams whose members play an active role in matter leadership and oversight.

6. Case assessment and scoping

At the outset of every new matter, the proposed team should be discussed, along with the scope of work to be performed and the budget. The client and firm will take into account the skills, level of experience and price point of the professionals involved. In-house lawyers, in particular, like to be involved in selecting attorneys who work on their matters – particularly if they are different from those who were present at the initial 'pitch' to the client.

7. Establish budgets and timelines

Once scoped and staffed, budgets should be prepared with milestones and benchmark metrics in place to monitor in real time. The firm and client should agree on how progress, status updates and timelines will be monitored and by whom – for example, a designated project manager – and when clients would like a 'red-flag' trigger for certain change orders, overages or other deviations from the initial scope and budget.

"You can only strengthen client loyalty if you continuously engage in meaningful dialogue with clients and receive specific insights into where and how you can improve and how you can better meet their needs."

IV. SEEKING CLIENT FEEDBACK AND INSIGHTS TO IMPROVE LONG-TERM LOYALTY

1. Introduction

You can only strengthen client loyalty if you continuously engage in meaningful dialogue with clients and receive specific insights into where and how you can improve and how you can better meet their needs. In today's hyper-competitive, fast-changing marketplace, it is critical to base strategic decisions and service delivery execution on the voice of the client.

Getting feedback and insights from clients allows firms to improve client satisfaction, enhance customer experience, appropriately respond to client needs – both challenges and opportunities – and address any concerns or issues that clients have about efficiency, effectiveness, communications, budgeting, work quality or service delivery. Occasionally, clients also express dissatisfaction or have interpersonal clashes with specific lawyers at the firm, including partners. This is vitally important to learn. Clients rarely complain when they are unhappy, despite partners insisting they do, and instead either gradually or suddenly take their work to other firms.

Establishing a robust client feedback programme reflects a deeper cultural value: that your firm wants to hear from clients, engage in dialogue and work together on continuous improvement. If your firm is truly committed to this value, it will have far-ranging implications across the board – for example, in relation to:

- the lawyers you hire;
- how you train and evaluate and reward partners, associates and staff;
- the investments you make in technology, knowledge management and other client-centric resources; and
- the approaches you take to create customised client service plans and protocols.

In essence, this is a mind-set, not a one-shot approach to marketing.

Anticipate the resistance and pushback that you will get from partners. The most frequent objections usually reflect:

- partners' desire to control relationships and not let others talk to 'their' client;
- a fear that clients will think there is something wrong if they are asked for feedback; and
- either an insecurity or arrogance that makes partners believe they already know what clients think or fear about any negative feedback they may share.

There really are only three key measures of client satisfaction I am interested in:

- *Did you achieve the stated objective and outcome?*
- *Were you efficient and did you meet the budget?*
- *What was my customer experience? What was it like to work with you?*

After-action reviews are our most important, yet least used tool. They are the basis upon which to have rich conversations between the provider and the customer. This is the basis for continuous improvement – to realise our vision that "The best legal problem is the one you never have." This is what creates stickiness.

When doing performance reviews with firms, I prefer to meet with the relationship partner/team leader. I ask the team leader to go first and talk about what the team could have done differently; then our team follows about what we could have done differently. This opens up a rich discussion and opportunities for improvement.

Jeff Carr
Former senior vice president and general counsel of Univar Solutions and FMC Technologies

Extremely satisfied clients who consistently give top ratings to a firm on multiple attributes demonstrate their loyalty. As we discussed in Part 2, Chapter II, an even more critical indicator of loyalty is a client's willingness and actual practice of endorsing and referring a firm to peers in the same company or colleagues in other companies. Historically, as much as 50% or 60% of a firm's new business comes from referrals from loyalist clients.

If law firms want to increase their revenue and profitability, having a formal and ongoing strategy for seeking and using client feedback must be a key focus of their growth strategy. Firms that aggressively pursue a client feedback programme together with a client account management strategy report significantly higher profits. Profits and growth are driven by loyal clients who routinely provide feedback that they are extremely satisfied, and whose firms are quick to address any areas that require attention or improvement. This last point is an important one, as firms that seek feedback but do not act on the information that clients share often do more damage to the relationship than if they had not solicited the feedback.

An important cautionary note: client feedback programmes should not be confused with cross-selling and sales efforts or other forms of market research. Too many firms go into client feedback meetings asking for more work in other areas before even establishing the level of satisfaction on existing work and service delivery. Only truly loyal clients will refer you to others, which is one of the critical questions to be asked at the end of an interview.

2. Client-initiated feedback on their firms

Even before the Association of Corporate Counsel's (ACC) Value Challenge initiative was launched in 2009, and certainly spurred on by this since then, many companies have begun their own internal satisfaction surveys, so that everyone on their internal teams has the opportunity and obligation to rate their lawyers and firms on a number of factors. For a while, the ACC even instituted its own rating system for the firms it used, which was shared only with other ACC members. This was quickly disbanded after much negative reaction on the part of firms and in-house lawyers; but in-house counsel have their own methods for sharing their opinions of their law firms. Many general counsel have instituted their own regular feedback programmes. One of the earliest and most effective was that developed by Jeff Carr, then senior vice president and general counsel of FMC Technologies (see Part 6, Chapter I for a detailed description of his ACES Model).

In around 2010, billing software and pricing vendors began building and sharing databases on the costs of certain services and the billing rates of all of the firms that in-house teams used which also utilised

"Too many firms go into client feedback meetings asking for more work in other areas before even establishing the level of satisfaction on existing work and service delivery."

their billing platforms. As the use of procurement professionals, panel competitions and RFPs increased, these became an important resource for analysing legal spend, law firm efficiency and overall price and value.

3. Types of feedback and methods of seeking client input
To be effective, client feedback must become part of every lawyer's and staff person's daily routine, not an annual or one-time event. This means that everyone should keep their ears open for expressions of concern or frustration on the part of a client, and should share them with others on the team. The methods for obtaining feedback range from the very formal – annual full-day audits with clients; satisfaction and assessment interviews; end-of-matter interviews or surveys; and online surveys – to less formal interactions by phone and email to gauge how things are going.

Some level of ongoing dialogue and feedback should be instituted for all clients of the firm. The more time consuming (for the firm and the client) should be reserved for priority clients, as determined by their revenue, longevity with the firm, strategic importance or some other criterion that has been agreed upon and articulated.

3.1 After-action reviews/end of matter surveys

This type of survey, often done digitally, is sent to clients at the conclusion of every matter or deal. If the matter is an extended litigation engagement or a major deal, these reviews should be done on the completion of key phases or milestones. You do not want to wait a year or two (which some litigation cases and deals that are put on hold can take).

After-action reviews are often done orally, in meetings in person or via videoconference. They must be kept at a clinical level, so that individuals neither blame nor get blamed for things that didn't go well. The purpose is to review frequently during an engagement so that adjustments and improvements can be made.

Sample after-action review questions include the following:

- What was our objective for the matter/deal/engagement?
- What was the actual outcome? How did this compare to articulated objectives, schedule, budget and initial assumptions?
- What went right and why?
- What went wrong and why?
- What have we learned?
- What will we do differently the next time?

3.2 Annual client feedback interviews

These are best done in person, when feasible, or by phone; clients should be given the option to choose. Prior to the 2020 COVID-19 pandemic, most clients were receptive to in-person meetings; but others still preferred to do them by phone. This interview is best done with someone other than the key engagement or relationship partner. While this may seem counterintuitive, clients are more likely to be candid about any concerns or issues they have if they don't have to tell the partner who is responsible for directly overseeing the relationship.

3.3 Annual client audit

Top clients of the firm (ie, those that generate 80% or more of its revenue) – and especially those for which the firm has established key client teams and/or is on preferred panels for – merit an in-depth meeting once a year or perhaps biannually. This requires an onsite visit, so that the law firm team can meet with various members of the in-house team, explore the client's plan or facilities, learn more about the business and even meet some of the company's executives in various business units. During the visit, respective members of the firm's and the client's operations teams (eg, billing, IT, pricing, procurement) might also meet to discuss improvements and collaboration.

The purpose of this more in-depth audit is to conduct a full assessment of how the client's needs are being met and how its needs may evolve in the future, based on trends, regulatory and economic forces, opportunities, growth strategy and business and legal risks. The objectives of these in-depth meetings are to further understand the client's business, hear from client representatives at various levels and strengthen the partnership together. At this meeting, the client and law firm will also review the service plan and the annual client team plans, and revise them as appropriate for the coming year.

3.4 Online surveys

These are best used with smaller clients and where the firm may be only representing an individual. The response rate of online surveys usually hovers around 15%; and clients are usually reluctant to put any complaints in writing and tend to score firms higher just so they won't be asked how the firm could improve. As clients should always be given the option to respond anonymously, completed surveys should be returned to the senior business development or marketing director, another senior administrative professional or the outside consultant, if used.

"The response rate of online surveys usually hovers around 15%; and clients are usually reluctant to put any complaints in writing and tend to score firms higher just so they won't be asked how the firm could improve."

3.5 Net Promoter Score®

Unlike online surveys, which are usually comprised of eight to 10 questions with a rating scale, each with space for comments, the Net Promoter Score® is a single question that can be sent to multiple people within the same client organisation once a year or at the end of a matter. (We reviewed this concept in Part 2, Chapter II in greater detail.)[7] While many law firms do not use this simple, single-question format as frequently, it can be a nice adjunct to other forms of feedback gathering. Some of the top legal services companies, such as Elevate, are building their brands on high customer satisfaction and regularly use the Net Promoter Score® as a way to measure and improve client satisfaction.

Firms that have put in place frequent and formal feedback programmes realise the substantial benefits. They use the information to improve and expand specific client relationships, but also to glean themes and lessons and suggestions that can be applied to other clients. Aggregated client feedback and trends can be used to:

- guide strategic plans;
- make wise decisions about investments such as technology, project management and even lateral hires; and
- help to train and evaluate the effectiveness of lawyers and staff in core competencies related to skills that clients deem important.

See Appendices III and IV for a roadmap on how to conduct effective client interviews and for sample client feedback questions to ask during an interview.

Part 4. Developing loyal client relationships

I. FROM EXPERT TO TRUSTED PARTNER AND BUSINESS ADVISER

1. Introduction

Most lawyers have developed deep areas of expertise within practice areas, client types and industries. This is a change from decades ago, when most rainmakers were generalists, able to personally satisfy many needs of clients – from contracts to litigation, from employment to real estate, tax and trusts and estates. But from the end of the last century to the present day, increasingly complex regulations, new laws and ever-changing business models and innovation have necessitated greater specialisation in order to service clients' specific and complex needs.

Unfortunately, many lawyers have become so specialised as subject-matter experts that they do not develop their skills and knowledge as broader business advisers; nor do they often understand what it is their colleagues do in other areas of practice. This limits their ability to engage in broader strategic discussions with clients about the relationship of legal issues to the business, and the inter-related nature and impact of various legal issues on a specific matter or deal.

Clients want their lawyers to be much more than experts in their fields.

The lawyers I have the most loyalty to are those that really understand the business problem, not just the legal problem. They give me a strategic assessment of the law and the facts, and suggest to us what we could gain or what we could lose if we follow a certain strategy. They focus on getting to a solution as efficiently and quickly as possible without sacrificing the outcome.

Maureen Harms
Associate general counsel and managing counsel, 3M Co

Led by businesses in the United Kingdom, many in-house counsel now expect their lawyers to be 'commercial'. This means much more than just knowing the business and industry that clients are in. It means having a deep understanding of the business itself: how products and services are produced or manufactured and marketed; their distribution channels; their financial, pricing and profit model; how the company makes money; its operational risks and risk tolerance; who its customers are; who its competitors are; and how its legal matters and approaches fit into its overall risk profile and/or strategy.

Perhaps more fundamentally, lawyers need to become solution providers. Too often, lawyers are risk averse: known as 'deal breakers', not deal makers; finding a problem for every solution instead of a solution for every problem. In-house departments are also trying to get their own lawyers out of their silos to better understand their companies as integrated businesses and become departments of 'know' instead of departments of 'no'.

Clients themselves – especially those in the general counsel or chief legal officer position – are also under great pressure to understand all aspects of the business, as they now often have a seat in the C-suite, and not just as leader of the legal department. Given the changing dynamic of both what is expected of clients themselves and what they now expect of their outside counsel, the skills profile of the successful lawyer has changed.

In order to earn the role of trusted adviser and business partner, lawyers need to add broader knowledge to their vertical expertise and be able to understand and comfortably discuss a client's organisation, business priorities and business model, industry, strategy, trends, regulation and economic impacts. Even more fundamentally, lawyers need to develop a 'learning mind-set' in which they seek out knowledge, are curious and open-minded, and don't make assumptions or jump too quickly to conclusions.

One of the most important aspects of building close relationships with clients is the ongoing sharing of knowledge and insights. This can also be described as 'intimacy'. Clients share confidential information as well as personal concerns about risks, threats and their company's health and stability; and lawyers share their knowledge of broader legal implications, business strategy and legal strategies. While lawyers used to 'hoard' information about legal processes for fear that their clients might use this themselves and no longer need their lawyers, clients rely on trusted advisers well beyond the legal matter or case at hand.

2. Lawyers need to shift from I-shaped to T-shaped in advice and skills

Decades ago, lawyers were generalists and more often served in an advisory role. They may have served as general counsel to companies, advising on everything from the corporate books and the boardroom to real estate and disputes. But as regulations became more complex in the 1970s, 1980s and 1990s, the need for specialisation and greater depth in specific areas drove lawyers to narrow their skills and become experts in their field. This was accelerated by clients, which began selecting lawyers on their track record of success and experience in specialised areas and industries. Lawyers developed deep expertise in a specialty along the vertical bar of a 'T' and hence, were 'I' shaped.[8]

Lawyers now need to shift from being I-shaped to T-shaped.[9] While there will still be a role for lawyers who are deep technical experts, those who wish to become trusted advisers and client relationship lawyers will require critical additional skillsets. The T-shaped professional embodies the skills that employers in many fields are pursuing, hiring and advancing.

T-shaped professionals have cross-disciplinary knowledge that is both broad and deep – they are experts in their field, but can also think broadly about other disciplines. I-shaped professionals have very deep, specialised knowledge in one or two disciplines, but limited – if any – knowledge or skill in other disciplines and characteristics. In law firms, many successful client relationship partners and rainmakers are T-shaped. The skills embodied in the horizontal bar of the T usually include:

- creativity and innovation;
- communication, including the ability to negotiate and collaborate;
- the ability to apply knowledge across disciplines;
- empathy, including the ability to put yourself in others' shoes and understand other cultures; and
- an understanding of substantive areas outside your area of expertise.

As technology continues to automate many tasks previously done by people, and as clients continue to use non-traditional legal service providers for work that is more routine, law firms will have to focus on the unique skills and benefits that their lawyers offer to clients. The need to provide clients with lawyers who embody these characteristics will impact on how law firms hire, train, advance and compensate their lawyers. It should also accelerate the recognition that those trained in other disciplines who often embody more of these skills – for example, HR, talent management (recruiting, training

Sometimes you do get problems that come up and you don't have enough experience on that type of issue. It can be helpful to turn to someone in the law firm who has been down that road a few times, and they can look at you and say, "Don't worry about it" or "That could be a problem." That kind of relationship is critical. There are some people who are really, really good at that. They've been in numerous boardrooms, have taken scores of companies public and have really good instincts about what's going to matter and what's not going to matter. Having a really good person like that at your side is really helpful sometimes.

Mark Chandler
Executive vice president, chief legal officer and chief compliance officer, Cisco Systems, Inc

and advancement), marketing and business development and knowledge management – should play a more prominent role in how firms are led and managed, and perhaps in the management of client relationships.

3. Transitioning from expert to adviser

In Part 3, Chapter I, we suggested that trust must be earned and is personal – between two people, not between a company and a law firm. It develops after multiple interactions in which you demonstrate your competence, skills and expertise and achieve favourable outcomes. It also comes as you develop and share more knowledge with clients and open yourself up to some vulnerability.

Being an adviser reflects a more advanced skillset and approach to working with clients. As an expert, you are hired for your technical knowledge and track record of getting results. Often in this type of relationship with a client, you have analysed and are providing the facts and case law, and telling the client how they should approach their issue. Most of the relationship is still at a professional level, although you may be developing professional trust.

We have found that the small boutique firms (fewer than 50 lawyers) often give us the best advice and value. They tend to be well managed and agile. They focus on providing us with strategic advice, not 'CYA' memos, and will give us their opinion on what we should do. They really understand us and are excellent at their area of expertise.

Associate general counsel, multinational company

To serve as a trusted adviser, however, you must have both depth in your area of expertise and knowledge of the client's business, industry and other issues that the client likely is dealing with. More time is spent asking good, thoughtful questions, listening to the answers and probing further. At this level, you are partnering with the client on issue spotting and problem solving, which will likely take you outside your practice area of expertise. Perhaps most importantly, clients rely on advisers for their insight, experience and judgement. At this point, relationships usually transcend a professional relationship and expand into a personal relationship.

4. The increasing importance of empathy and listening

Becoming a trusted adviser and business partner to clients often begins with doing great work for them and providing superb service. Even from the outset, however, lawyers who earn client trust and loyalty have and demonstrate high levels of empathy. The most fundamental aspects of empathy are the ability to truly understand the client's perspective, including their feelings, needs and concerns. Being empathetic requires exceptional listening skills and the foresight to ask the questions that will elicit the information needed to better understand a client's needs – often before they are even aware of those needs themselves.

While an expert often listens and advises with the head, the adviser/partner listens and advises with the head (expertise) and the heart (empathy and understanding.) They listen not just to what is said, but also to what is meant and conveyed through non-verbal messages. They understand a client's communication style and motivations. Advisers don't engage in one-way conversations, but do more listening than talking and discern the dimensions of what a client is dealing with, including internal political and professional challenges and realities.

At its core, empathy requires selflessness, self-awareness and genuine interest in helping the client. While advisers come across as being spontaneous, most come to conversations well prepared, having reviewed recent notes and updates, conducted some up-to-date research on the company and industry, and checked in with team members and other advisers to the client.

Attributes of the best lawyer advisers

Clients who trust lawyers for more than the legal matters for which they or their firms were hired want advice and help in thinking about the bigger issues and opportunities that will affect their success. This requires lawyers to be T-shaped, as discussed previously in this chapter. The best and most trusted partner advisers also:

- fully explore, understand and distil a client's broader goals and context;
- stay focused on the client's needs and agenda, and are genuinely interested in helping the client to succeed;
- continuously keep a finger on the pulse of issues and trends that might affect the client, and proactively reach out to brief the client and provide insights and considerations;
- stay abreast of what the client's peers and competitors are doing, and bring that market intelligence to the client;
- maintain full communication and coordination within the client team, keeping everyone abreast of current matters, client concerns and any issues that the team has spotted or is concerned about on the client's behalf;
- make the client feel truly valued and appreciated;
- have the client's back and make the client look good to their peers, executives and the board;
- regularly spend time off the clock, fielding calls from the client and ensuring that things are running smoothly both with the client team in the firm and with the client's team; and
- frequently meet with the client on open matters and serve as a sounding board for any internal, political or personal concerns that the client may have.

II. DEVELOPING AND NURTURING LONG-TERM RELATIONSHIPS

1. Introduction

Too often, clients are taken for granted or viewed merely as a source of revenue. Firms focus on getting new matters, cross-selling and pitching, often without much attention to what clients really need or want, or to the relationship itself. Relationships with clients must be nurtured in many of the same ways as important personal relationships. While so much energy often goes into 'the chase' of landing a new client or new matter, bringing in a new client should be just the beginning of the romance, not the beginning of the end. Clients want to be assured every day that they made the right choice in choosing your firm to help them with their legal problems. Make sure that you are doing this by becoming a close and trusted adviser.

2. Work on the personal relationship

With all the pressures that clients are under to reduce legal fees, use procurement officers and ask firms to bids on cases through RFPs, it is easy to forget that clients have a human side and that personal relationships still often count for more than might appear. Don't wait until after a matter has concluded to begin to get to know the client. At the beginning or end of every call or meeting, initiate some personal conversation – off the clock, of course!

"While so much energy often goes into 'the chase' of landing a new client or new matter, bringing in a new client should be just the beginning of the romance, not the beginning of the end."

Take time to reach out to clients and get to know what motivates them, what is important to them and how they spend their time outside of the office. Finding commonalities and mutual interests is a good way to deepen bonds with a client. This might be where you grew up; college or law school; hobbies such as golf, tennis, painting, running marathons, sports teams, gardening, the performing or visual arts; favourite travel spots and restaurants; and charitable and civic activities about which you or they are passionate. Listen for clues about their personal lives to see whether you can offer to help in any way – for example, by sharing insights with a child considering career options; offering to write a letter of recommendation or referral; or finding tickets to highly sought after concerts or sporting events.

Spend a little time every day thinking about clients outside of current/active matters. You need to dedicate at least one to two hours a week to connecting and reconnecting with key clients by phone and in person. Don't forget that face time is still the most effective way to keep a relationship going if you are able to do so (see also the following chapter on nurturing relationships remotely).

At year's end, send a handwritten note of thanks and a small gift (if your clients can accept them – many cannot). Many send a donation in the client's name to an organisation. This is best done when the organisation is something that the individual client is passionate about. It is important to let clients know that you appreciate their trust in you and their business. Write down every client's birthday (and other known special occasions, such as their wedding anniversary or anniversary of business) on your calendar. Make a call or write a note/card for each special day.

3. Stay top of mind as a resource and business adviser
Clients appreciate someone who is genuinely interested in their success and seems to keep them on their radar at all times. Set up a Google alert or use other tools to track client news about their business, promotions, new offices and products, stock activity and so on. Send them emails or give them a call when you come across this news. Monitor the business and legal activities of your clients' competitors. Where possible, share insights and case studies. Arm them with 'intelligence' before they need it and provide some suggestions – even better if this is useful information that your contact can share with other executives in the C-suite. This will make your contact look smart and strategic.

Further your understanding of the client's business and the way it operates. Go and spend a day or two with the client at their place of business (on your own time/dime.) Ask to follow others around, sit in on meetings and meet others on the business side. This investment of time will be appreciated by clients, and will provide you and your team with a much better sense of what the business is about and how the legal team interacts with the business. If possible, offer to attend board meetings.

Get to know key client team members, including assistants and other important professionals, and their contact information. Add all relevant contacts to your client team and firm email lists. Designate client contacts to receive firm mailings, announcements and blogs/alerts. Acknowledge a good job by someone you work with at the client's organisation by mentioning or writing a note to his or her superior.

4. Be likeable and genuine

If you are not a naturally outgoing person, work on becoming someone whom others can talk to and relate to. Consider whether you come across as haughty or arrogant, and don't take yourself too seriously – something that lawyers can easily do. When interacting with clients, especially on non-matter related topics, focus on listening, not talking, and focus on the client, including his or her needs, interests and questions. Be genuine in your interest and listen without interrupting. Bring humour and friendliness to the relationship.

Identify clients whom you would like to entertain once things open up again (keep in mind that some clients prefer to focus only on their business relationship and limit time to meetings and phone conversations). Find out what your client enjoys and whether their preference is to do something with their spouse or family or with other colleagues. Do not make gender assumptions about whether certain clients will or will not enjoy sporting or arts events.

5. Communication, communication, communication

Something that clients still complain about is that their lawyers do not communicate with them often enough or are not clear or transparent in their communication. This aspect of the relationship is critical to forming deep trust and conveying reliability. Always err on the side of communicating too frequently, but be sure to ask clients how often they want to hear from you, especially on the status of matters. Do they want to be copied or bcc'd on every email? In which decisions and meetings do they want to be involved? For example, would they appreciate a brief 15-minute status call every week or two on the same day and time?

Clients often become unhappy when their lawyers wait too long to let them know of a problem, a change in staffing or a budget overage. These are the kinds of 'surprises' that clients really dislike. Transparency and honesty are always the best way to communicate with clients. Phone calls and meetings should be followed up with notes and next steps within 48 hours, to ensure that everyone is on the same page.

6. Accessibility and responsiveness

Try to answer calls personally when you can, rather than relying on your assistant or voicemail. Do not over-screen your calls or give the impression that you are too busy to talk to the client. Keep your calendar up to date and share it with or make it accessible to your assistant and other attorneys, so that they know when you are tied up, when you will be free and who else they should call in your absence. Keep your assistant informed about the status of activities and how you would like him or her to respond when you are on calls, in meetings or in court.

Always return phone calls and emails within four to six hours or by the end of the business day, and call clients at home if necessary. If you cannot return a call or email on the same day, at least let the client know that you received their email or voicemail and will get back to them that evening or the next day. Try to establish the relative urgency and priority of clients' needs. When do they need an answer – today? Within the hour? Within the week? Can anyone else help? Call clients and let them know when you have been able to complete a task for them that has some urgency.

7. Co-marketing with clients

Remember that clients are often looking for ways to increase their own visibility and credibility, and often don't get recognition for their knowledge, skills and ideas. They need this visibility and recognition – as you do – for professional advancement, satisfaction and a sense of accomplishment. Think about and discuss with your clients opportunities to host or sponsor an event or webinar on an issue of legal or general interest. Promote it through publicity and through your LinkedIn pages (your personal page and the firm's page). Have it recorded and invite groups of other clients to view the presentation over lunch or breakfast (or via videoconference on Zoom, Webex or Microsoft Meetings).

Ask clients what business and industry publications they read and explore whether they would like to co-author an article with you in a trade or business publication. Identify opportunities to give presentations to industry associations or business groups such as the Association for Corporate Growth or a chamber of commerce. Ask your client(s) to serve on the panel with you. Interview them and quote them in articles or LinkedIn posts (with their permission, of course).

8. Client advisory boards

With so much change occurring in the legal profession, it is essential that law firms engage in active and ongoing dialogue with clients to assess needs and understand their critical business goals and priorities. Getting input directly from the marketplace – those who purchase the firm's services – is critical to a law firm's strategic planning efforts. One way to ensure that a firm is receiving the kind of insights and feedback it needs is to form a client advisory board. This group of six to eight clients meets regularly and serves as a sounding board on issues of importance to the law firm. It operates in a similar manner to a corporate board of directors.

It is important to establish and articulate clear objectives for the board and then to carefully select members. Effective board members will represent a diverse range of skills, including finance, technology, marketing and customer service, operations and HR. You will likely include clients from a few different industries and those who represent your current or future 'ideal' client type. You want to include clients who have a very positive view of your firm, but who will be candid and open with their feedback and insights.

Once your client board members have been identified and invited to join, you need to design and publish a structure for meetings and ongoing communication. Expectations should be transparent. Some firms hold their meetings on a quarterly or semi-annual basis. Preferably, these are held in person. Clients, if out of town, are flown in and hosted at a nice hotel. Often the meetings run a full day, or from late afternoon through dinner and the morning of the next day. Agendas should be carefully planned with any necessary background information and sent to board members a week or two in advance.

III. MAINTAINING AND DEEPENING CLIENT RELATIONSHIPS REMOTELY

1. Introduction

The COVID-19 pandemic of 2020 had a major impact on all aspects of life and the economy. The most radical shift was the mandate to socially distance and work remotely. Offices were closed, conferences and other business events cancelled, and court proceedings suspended, followed by the implementation of online pre-trial depositions, negotiations and mediations.

This radical change in how lawyers execute legal work has had a similar impact on lawyers' methods of client interaction, entertainment and relationship building. Not being able to meet with clients on case-specific matters, provide on-site continuing legal education (CLE) opportunities, see each other at conferences and enjoy social outings together has eliminated the in-person opportunities to develop relationships organically and made it more difficult to find commonalities with clients on a personal and professional level.

Lawyers should be prepared for the possibility that business will not return to pre-pandemic norms, in that many businesses may permanently offer employees remote working options and may curtail travel on the part of their own employees and lawyers who want to attend meetings or conferences in person. Clients are already indicating that they are unlikely to want to pay for lawyers to fly in for meetings. Even prior to the pandemic, companies were beginning to cut travel and conference budgets of their in-house lawyers and business directors. If this happens, lawyers will need to develop alternative methods of deepening and expanding relationships remotely.

During a pandemic or other crisis in which businesses are dramatically disrupted and everyone is experiencing a lot of stress, the best things that lawyers can provide to their clients are care, comfort, trust, security and humaneness. This is a time for more frequent outreach to ask, listen and see how you can help. In his famous book *How to Win Friends and Influence People*, Dale Carnegie says, "To be interesting, you must be interested."[10] Clients really need you to be interested in them, especially in times of stress and disruption.

Dr Albert Mehrabian was among the first experts to suggest that the various factors involved in communication can be broken down as follows: 7% spoken words, 38% tone of voice and 55% body language.[11] What you say matters much less than the tone and tempo of your voice. According to Dr Mehrabian and others, over half of how people communicate and are perceived is through body language: posture, facial expressions, hand gestures, eye contact, dress, grooming and others. This is why remote communication makes it more difficult to build rapport and trust; and why communicating via video conference and video chatting is the best alternative to meeting and interacting in person.

Videoconferencing has become a reasonable substitute for in-person meetings, but it is less effective than in-person communication in a number of ways:

- Meetings have to be scheduled and almost never can be spontaneous, and they tend to follow a tighter agenda, with little room for side conversations.
- While viewers can see each other – their facial expressions, body language and attire – the size of the picture is small if there are multiple people in the meeting and technology can be problematic (eg, unclear images, delays in sound or video, echoes, dropped calls).
- Working from home can lead to interruptions from family members, pets and other distractions.
- There is no opportunity for physical contact, such as a handshake.
- It is more difficult to engage in 'small talk', catch up on personal news and build rapport.

A word of caution: people can tire of meeting via videoconference, whether in a work context or in an effort to replicate cocktail hours, book clubs and so on. It can feel overdone and intrusive, so clients should be given the option to meet with a video option, but not forced to do so. There may be some instances where you are on video, but the client elects to turn off the video; it may still be advantageous for the client to see you even if you cannot see the client.

Even before the pandemic forced people to work and interact remotely, one of the most effective ways of connecting with clients has always been by phone. However, too often, lawyers – especially millennials – are uncomfortable reaching out by phone. Everyone is now so accustomed to emailing and texting that the benefits of communicating by phone are often lost. As with video, where clients can see you and hear you, phone calls are a better alternative than email for checking in, deepening rapport and often more quickly conveying questions or concerns. Emails can be misunderstood or written poorly. They are often used when people feel uncomfortable disagreeing with someone or want to be on record for a point or clarification. Sometimes, email exchanges get heated and things then can be misinterpreted, exaggerated or misconstrued.

Nothing can replace the effectiveness and desirability of building relationships face to face. Despite the agility and resilience that lawyers and their clients demonstrated in response to the COVID-19 crisis, it will always be more effective to develop genuine rapport and trust when people can spend some time together that allows for casual conversation, personal story sharing and the development of commonalities and connection. Fortunately, there are ways to nurture and deepen relationships even when one cannot do so in person.

2. Steps to build rapport and closer relationships remotely

- Schedule video calls/meetings on a regular (but not too regular) basis – it is important to see people, their reactions and their body language, and it will help to maintain some closeness and intimacy.
- Pay attention to any signals or indicators that the client is stressed, or for special events and interests. Not being able to be together means you may have to supplement by occasionally sending a bottle of wine or something else of personal interest.
- Become comfortable with and proficient in videoconferencing: dress professionally; set up a room that resembles a tidy office space; get the right backlighting; invest in a good headset; smile and look into the camera; don't appear distracted. Even if some in the meeting have their video turned off, keep yours on.
- Make sure that every video meeting is interactive – consider using the whiteboarding feature to allow collaborative brainstorming.
- Begin every call/meeting with a personal catch-up – how the weekend went; how the family is doing; recent holidays; career updates (if the client is looking to advance or change companies). Finish the meeting with another personal message.
- Replicate as best you can some of the kinds of social interactions you would be having if you were able to do so in person – for example, Zoom cocktail hours, a coffee, a wine tasting or a sports trivia night.
- If you have not spoken with a client in a while and have been unable to see them in person, pick up the phone; and if the client is unavailable, leave a voice message. Clients will appreciate hearing your voice.
- Get and stay more active on social media – share insights; comment on articles or others' posts; be an active participant in LinkedIn Groups.
- Stay in touch by phone, text or email more deliberately and frequently on both matter/deal-related topics and those of general interest; there is a greater risk of 'out of sight, out of mind' when you cannot see 10 or 20 key contacts at a time at a conference, where there is ample time for socialising and connecting. Add ticklers to your calendar if you are not already speaking with your client several times a week.

- Become an excellent listener with the intent to learn and show empathy. Given the tendency for remote meetings to be more formal and more stringent on time restrictions, this can make you feel more pressure to follow an agenda. Even if focusing on specific issues related to a matter, be sure to ask good questions and listen for both the answers and the feelings.
- Continue to seek feedback from the client on how you and your team are performing the work, getting the results and delivering exceptional service. This will also require you to do more frequent scheduled team calls, to ensure that other lawyers and staff can support the client at a superior service level.
- Host online CLE training, webinars and learning sessions for clients – both for the lawyers and for their administrative personnel.
- Consider hosting smaller, more regular discussion groups that pull together clients with similar issues and challenges to discuss them.
- Host social events on Zoom or whatever platform you use to try to provide a more personal and fun forum to get to know each other and clients with similar interests. You might host a wine and spirits night with a sommelier, a cooking class with a known chef, a trivia night or a Zoomtail evening.

Even when in-person meetings resume, and certainly when you cannot meet in person, remember to use the telephone and videoconferencing. Clients can at least hear your voice and see you on video. It feels more personal and is more direct, and questions or concerns can more easily be addressed in real time. Client relationships require ongoing attention and nurturing, using a variety of methods that address the multiple dimensions and interests that clients have.

IV. ADDRESSING CHALLENGING OR DIFFICULT CLIENTS

1. Introduction

As we noted in Part 2, Chapter II, you will not have deep, trusting and successful relationships with all of your clients. When you think of your 'ideal' or favourite clients, you may designate them as such in part because the work is challenging; they are in a growth industry; they are acquisitive and innovative; and/or they never argue about your fees. But an important consideration is how well you and your client relate and interact; whether there is chemistry, commonality, mutual respect and likeability.

In the legal profession, clients are often considered demanding and increasingly they are putting pressure on their law firms to do much more for much less. Technology now enables connectivity 24/7; and given the high hourly rates that many clients pay their lawyers, they somehow have come to expect their lawyers to be available to them at all hours and to turn work product around in often unrealistic timeframes.

There are a number of different types of difficult clients that lawyers often encounter:

- Everything is a crisis: These are clients who treat everything they do and ask you to do as an emergency, always running around with their hair on fire.
- Rude and disrespectful: These clients often seem to be on the attack and overly critical, picking apart every email and memo, looking for errors and ways to 'one-up' the lawyer. It is not uncommon for them to yell on the phone, berate you and cause associates or staff to cry.
- Demanding and unreasonable: These clients email their lawyer late on a Friday and ask for turnaround over the weekend, or email relentlessly throughout the weekend, requesting additional input or asking new questions that may not be critical, but for which they still want an immediate response.
- "I'm smarter than you are": These are clients who seem to resent the fact that they must work with outside lawyers and constantly question your advice, conclusions or recommendations. They second guess everything that you propose and minimise any help that you provide. They may also micromanage at a level that makes it difficult to get things done.
- Constantly push back on rates and fees: Even when firms have gone the extra mile to reduce fees, develop alternative pricing methods and provide a lot of additional value add-ons at no

extra charge, there are clients that question every single invoice, nit-pick on every hour billed and every person's recording time, and almost never pay a bill in full.

- Defer and procrastinate: These are clients who cannot seem to make a decision on anything without running it by several other people, and may take days or weeks to get back to you on something that they had said was urgent, so you turned around immediately.

Obviously, many clients may exhibit some aspects of these traits at different times during the relationship or engagement. Some of them will reflect the client's own levels of stress and how their managers are placing pressure and expectations on their work product and deliverables. Over time, you and the firm will have to determine whether you want to continue to work with clients who are consistently difficult, perhaps even abusive. Some clients clearly will not be a good fit for you or your firm. Many other clients who may be difficult might deserve some attention and effort to see whether the relationship and mode of interaction can be improved.

There are a number of steps that you and others on your team can take when dealing with difficult clients.

2. Let clients vent and stay calm

Often, in pressured situations, people need to blow off steam. A client's anger may be directed at you correctly or should actually be directed at someone else. Sometimes letting them express their anger and frustration, and listening without getting defensive, is the best way to settle them down. They need to know that you are listening and hearing what is on their minds. It can be difficult not to get defensive when you are receiving a barrage of criticism and disrespect; and at some point, if it becomes a pattern, this could be enough to conclude that the relationship is not a healthy one for you.

3. Put a little distance between heated exchanges

One of the mistakes that people make during or after an angry or critical interaction is to respond emotionally in the moment – to be defensive and strike out to dispute the other person's criticism. This is particularly true when you have been caught off guard and feel that you are being targeted unfairly. This often leads to over-reaction and things being said that shouldn't be said. It is best to let things sit for an hour or two, or even overnight, before you respond; but do be sure to respond quickly. Don't let things fester for a day or two. Be careful too of how much is exchanged in an email, as you cannot erase what has been written. After an exchange of two emails that seem to be leading to misperceptions, untruths or accusations, the best step is to pick up the phone and call the other person.

4. Apologise even if you didn't do anything wrong
Apologising doesn't mean that you have to admit to wrongdoing; it may simply be to let the client know that whatever transpired or whatever the transgression, you are sorry that they feel frustrated or let down. Using empathy and trying to be kind and gentle in your response to their rants can help to calm them down and help the conversation become more constructive and productive.

5. Don't throw your colleagues under the bus
It is difficult to hear criticism about your service or work product. When others have been involved in the matter and the client is being highly critical of something that your colleague did, it is easy to agree with the client first, apologise and then go and talk to your colleague. But a client can be wrong and unreasonable, and throwing your colleague under the bus before understanding what transpired will do serious damage that relationship. Again, your first step is to acknowledge the client's anger and frustration and assure them that you will look into it and get back to them.

6. Reset relationship expectations
Occasionally, ongoing unpleasant exchanges with clients mean that the client and lawyer are not in sync on their expectations of each other. If the client and lawyer have not established expectations upfront about deadlines, channels of communication, preferences for how work is completed and deliverables, it is unsurprising that the client may end up unhappy with how the lawyer is performing. As discussed in Part 3, Chapter III, establishing expectations and service protocols at the outset of a new client relationship can help to avert these types of issues. Even after you have begun working with a client, you can always modify the engagement letter if there is any residual confusion about mutual protocols. Perhaps most importantly, set aside time once or twice a year to talk to the client about what is working and not working within the relationship.

7. Consult with others
In some instances, you will need to bring a firm leader, practice group leader or client relationship partner into the situation. It may be that the client has a legitimate concern or complaint about your work product or your judgement; or you may feel that you cannot adequately assuage the client's complaints yourself. Rather than go it alone and risk your own emotional wellbeing or put the client relationship in jeopardy, it is always good to seek 'cover' and help from others.

8. Pull the plug
In some instances, difficult clients are harmful to the lawyer's health, the firm's reputation and the firm's financial bottom line. If you have

done all you can to try to address a client's unhappiness and anger, but the pattern of disrespect and unreasonableness continues, the client likely is not a good fit for your firm. As discussed previously, clients who are constantly angry and critical are saboteurs – they are likely out criticising you and the firm to their peers and may even be using social media to do so. We also know that when the squeaky wheel gets all the grease, it likely means that we are not spending enough time and attention with our most loyal clients or those that could be.

If you do decide to end a relationship with a client, try to do so gracefully and diplomatically if possible. You can suggest that the firm has moved in a different direction; that the firm may have outgrown the client in its fee structure; or that your respective ways of interacting are at odds with each other. If possible, refer them to another lawyer you think would be a good fit and do not speak badly of the client to others.

"For client teams to be effective, partners with relationships must be willing to share, collaborate and invest in the team process."

V. CLIENT ACCOUNT MANAGEMENT AND KEY CLIENT TEAMS

Customer loyalty is a critical focus. The approach firms are using to put together strategic client teams that help push this forward is a priority. Having the right blend of partners, associates and allied professionals on the team usually lends itself to a more successful outcome. Those that are doing a good job at developing clients by building relationships help avoid account volume erosion and organically build loyalty. They build institutional connections within the law firms and with the client.

Vincent Cordo
Former central legal operations officer and global sourcing officer, Shell Oil Co; now client development and relationship officer, Holland & Knight

1. Introduction

Client account management is a business strategy that law firms can use to think strategically about their important clients and formally monitor and address client needs, satisfaction, service and delivery, and opportunities for deepening and expanding the relationship. Key account management is a systematic approach that focuses on building loyal partnerships with a small number of significant clients in order to ensure the strategic development and retention of these key assets over the long term by achieving mutual goals and value.

Client account management requires ongoing oversight, leadership and execution, and for this reason is seldom embraced by law firms. Instead, most law firms have borrowed client account management principles from their corporate counterparts and have developed client service teams or key client teams to serve important clients. After over two decades of operating key client teams, firms are improving their understanding of them and their effectiveness at managing them. Early efforts saw too great a focus on using these teams primarily to grow their own profits by selling more services to key clients than they did on building long-term relationships that responded to current needs and co-created value.

Key client teams are important ways to improve client retention by increasing client satisfaction, trust and loyalty through better and more efficient service, coordination and communication, management and relationship development; and by providing expanded and multi-disciplinary service solutions to better meet the evolving needs of clients. For client teams to be effective, partners with relationships must be willing to share, collaborate and invest in the team process.

Some account management models are built around the concept of a single point of contact – someone at the law firm whom the client can call at any time. This could be the billing or relationship partner, or a designated client ombudsman for problems or concerns. What is critical in instances where multiple lawyers and practice groups are serving a client is for all team members to be in sync on communications, approaches and budgeting, strategy, status and client satisfaction.

Client teams must clearly articulate their objectives, which will include:

- gaining a more thorough understanding of the client's business: its strategy, commercial and operational model, customer base and distribution channels, revenue and profit model, business risk and legal priorities, and current unmet and future needs;

- increasing knowledge of the client's industry, competitors, regulatory and legal pressures, and economic trends and threats;
- identifying other law firms and service providers that the client uses, both to understand how the client differentiates and perceives your firm, and to explore opportunities to collaborate in the client's best interest;
- improving internal communication, knowledge and coordination so that all those serving the client – including administrative personnel – stay current on client contacts, preferences for service delivery, current open matters, recent meetings, CLE and other meaningful client interactions and future needs and opportunities;
- proactively identifying and addressing client needs in the practice areas for which the firm has been hired, but also others;
- enhancing mutual value by improving service efficiencies through automation, downward delegation and leverage, better budgeting and process management, meeting client budgets, adding value and managing work profitably;
- ensuring integration and continuity of lawyers serving the client, including laterals and new associates;
- improving overall coordination and client management;
- evaluating and improving consistency in how work is managed and billed, how key personnel interact with clients and the quality of work, regardless of which lawyers, support personnel and office or practice groups interact with the client; and
- instituting continuous feedback and improvement mechanisms, both to collect client feedback and to systematically address and institute changes.

While most companies have mature customer account management processes in place, law firms lag behind and are not structured or used to investing in 'extra' time or resources to help manage client relationships. As firms have come to realise how critical it is to work collaboratively to retain and grow existing clients, many have initiated client team programmes and hired dedicated client managers to oversee major client accounts. There are a number of considerations to ensure an effective client account management effort.

2. Be selective about the clients for which you choose to form a client team

This will depend on the size of your firm and the support available to help you manage the teams. For many firms, this might mean creating only five or 10 teams per year. The revenue that your firm receives from clients is important, but is not the only criterion – selected clients must value and be committed to building a long-term partnership with your firm. Begin by looking at your top 50 to 100 clients by revenue with an eye towards those from which you receive less than 10% or

"As firms have come to realise how critical it is to work collaboratively to retain and grow existing clients, many have initiated client team programmes and hired dedicated client managers to oversee major client accounts."

20% of their legal spend. Consider other clients that have strategic value – for example:

- clients that have selected you for their preferred provider panel;
- clients with name brands;
- newer clients that fit your 'ideal client' profile, but from which you are currently getting only one-off transactions;
- clients in industries on an aggressive growth path; and
- clients in growth/acquisition mode.

It is also vital to have a relationship partner who is willing to 'share' the client, share information and spend the time necessary to oversee the team initiative.

3. Define the role of the client team leader

In order to ensure consistency in approach and execution from one client team to the next, client team leaders should follow a 'job description' that articulates expectations and responsibilities. The relationship partner may already be doing many of these things, but not all. Some chafe at structure and accountability, but these are required for an effective client team. From broader responsibilities to more specific, these include:

- managing the team to ensure collaboration, coordination, planning and communication;
- establishing (with the client) and ensuring that the team follows client-specific service standards; and
- monitoring in real time a financial dashboard of all client matters to track budgets, staffing, profitability and utilisation.

Once there is a regular system of feedback, the team leader will discuss and act on feedback from clients. Finally, depending on the number of partners who are responsible for different work streams or engagements, the team leader may serve as ombudsman for the client and will also provide regular status updates to the management committee and perhaps other client team leaders.

4. Begin with a focus on the client
Conduct internal and external research, collect data and develop a central internal repository of information about the client, including:

- the backgrounds of key players and decision makers (including legal operations and procurement department personnel);
- an organisational chart of executives and the backgrounds and news on the same;
- an organisational chart of the legal department;
- the client's culture, values, reputation and messaging;
- key firm relationships with contacts at the client;
- lawsuits and deals, including size, amounts, outcomes and whether they were represented by a law firm or handled them internally;
- competitors/other law firms representing the client: types and amount of work, nature of relationship;
- news clippings, press releases and social media postings;
- three-year revenue data by practice area, adjusted for revenue generated strictly by rate increases versus new/expanded work, and an analysis of the type of work;
- the names of other important outside advisers, including certified public accountants, auditors, banks, investment banks and management consultants;
- annual reports, regulatory agency-required reports for public companies and other financial information;
- a review of its website, products, locations, alliances and marketing strategies;
- its primary competitors; and
- industry analysis.

Once you have collected what you can internally and have reviewed it, the next step is to conduct a satisfaction and needs assessment interview or a more comprehensive service audit with multiple people at the client, to see how the firm is doing in serving its needs. Ascertain company needs, industry needs, goals and relationship preferences. These meetings can be called 'value creation sessions'. It is a good idea at this early stage to let the client know that you are putting together a client management team, to see whether the client is receptive and has any preliminary suggestions. You want them to partner with you on this.

Additionally, you may want to distribute an internal survey to all of those timekeepers in the firm who have spent 100 hours or more per year working on client matters, as well as to key relationship partners who may not bill as many hours, but have frequent and high-level contacts with the client. The internal questionnaire should explore the following:

- the internal assessment of needs;
- the internal political and decision-making structure;
- the depth and breadth of relationships;
- key issues, threats and opportunities for the client; and
- key challenges, threats and opportunities for the firm.

5. Assess relationship strength vertically and horizontally
In any client relationship, but especially those between larger companies or organisations and mid to large-sized law firms, there are typically numerous important contacts that play a role in or impact on the success of engagements and the relationship. Once you have made a list of the executives, in-house lawyers, legal operations team, functional operations managers, executive assistants and all other primary and secondary decision makers and influencers at the client, you should list those in the firm who know these contacts, along with a rating on the strength of the relationship.

Moving from the bow-tie model to the diamond model could be a better client management approach.[12] Traditionally, major client relationships were controlled by the top rainmaker or billing partner, and all interactions and communications had to be channelled through that individual. The concept in the diamond model is that people at different seniority and functional levels with the firm and the client tend to communicate directly with each other (or at least they should), as opposed to having all communications channelled through a single point of contact. Recognising this helps firms to match their resources to the client contacts and identify any gaps; it also facilitates the development of trusting relationships across the spectrum of personnel and ensures that as people move up the career ladders, they stay connected with their peers.

Having so many concurrent relationships and interactions, however,

"Most key client teams meet for an hour on a monthly basis, but bi-monthly or quarterly might suffice if you have good reporting, recording and shared knowledge bases established."

necessitates that firms have real-time, digital methods to capture all relationship interactions (eg, through a customer relationship management (CRM) system) and engage in regular team communications through group emails and team meetings. It also means that, whether the client team employs a single or several designated key points of contact model, it will still be essential to coordinate and oversee all work for large clients. This could be accomplished through key client managers and/or matter responsible partners.

6. Select team members

This is perhaps the most difficult aspect of putting a client team together. In large firms, for their largest clients, there can be as many as five, 10 or even 20 separate work streams, with dozens of senior partners and hundreds of lawyers and staff involved. In general, the most effective size for teams is between five and 10 primary members. If large numbers of partners and associates are servicing the client in multiple practice specialties, select a primary member from each practice area, who then convenes a sub-team meeting on a quarterly basis and feeds back to the core team.

To help determine who has had the most active matter interaction, look at the last three years' billings to see which attorneys have been doing work for the client (above a certain level) – if multiple lawyers are from the same practice team, select a primary partner from each team. Often, this is not the relationship partner or billing partner, but rather a partner or associate with matter or practice area responsibility. If the firm utilises department business managers or a client account manager, this person should be included on the team, along with one or two associates who spend more than 100 hours a year with the client.

7. Establish team protocols and an internal communications plan
Once you have selected your clients and designated client team leaders and members, the next step is to establish a framework for ongoing communication, status updates and knowledge sharing; and more broadly, how the work of the team will be conducted, by whom and when. For example, how often will the team meet? Who will prepare the agendas and lead the meetings, write up and disseminate the meeting notes and follow-up actions, and store the notes on a shared internal site? Most key client teams meet for an hour on a monthly basis, but bi-monthly or quarterly might suffice if you have good reporting, recording and shared knowledge bases established. An administrative component includes:

- compiling and updating a client contact chart with names, phone numbers, emails and an internal firm team email list;
- scheduling meetings on Zoom or Webex, or in person;
- maintaining the centralised repository (electronic and paper) of client information, documents, the client's engagement and billing terms requirements;
- checking websites, social media and news; and
- keeping the team updated.

Many firms have now developed internal sites on their intranets that are accessible at least to all partners, and in some instances to all approved associates and staff too. These client-specific 'micro-sites' include information on:

- revenues and matters that the firm has worked on for the client;
- lawyers who have relationships with contacts at the client and have worked on matters (this is often fed through the CRM system, an enterprise relationship management system and billing); and
- all publicly available information, news and reports about the client, such as new executive or legal department hires, promotions, newly launched products and offices, acquisitions, client intelligence reports and industry news.

Having this available in a user-friendly format allows all lawyers to access this when they have an opportunity related to the client, to see what else the firm is doing, which lawyers have the best contacts and so on. Each client site requires continuous updating and editing, to ensure that the information is up to date and accurate.

8. Establish measurable goals and design and execute an annual action plan

Once the preliminary foundational research has been conducted and collected, and the initial client interviews completed, the team should hold several planning meetings (this will require several hours). During these meetings, the team will discuss highlights of the client information collected and conduct a SWOT analysis (strengths, weaknesses, opportunities and threats) of the firm's relationship with the client. Following this preliminary review, the team will devise 12-month goals. These should include some financial metrics around how to grow more business and how to become more profitable and efficient in servicing the client, as well as less quantitative objectives relating to service and to relationship depth and breadth.

The plan should address various aspects of your proposed client account management approach, including sections and specific steps that address:

"If clients feel that they have helped you to develop a joint plan for success, they will be much more invested in helping you to succeed."

- service protocols, pricing, budgeting and billing;
- who will be on the team for the client and the firm; and
- with whom and how the client should communicate concerns or problems.

The plan will include specifics about needs that the client is already using you for, as well as other potential needs that the firm is alert to and can proactively reach out to offer insights or observations on.

Perhaps most important is the component of the plan for how the client will receive ongoing information and communication on the following:

- one central contact per body of work/practice engagement;
- a chart of all important client contacts and key targets (using relationship depth analysis)
- the assignment of a primary firm contact for each client contact (including associates);
- service protocols – for example, messages when attorneys are unavailable, returning phone calls, back-up during holidays and business trips;
- engagement letters for new matters;
- end-of-matter feedback surveys;
- status reports and conferences on all open matters; and
- project steps, budgeting and tracking.

The key to executing on an effective client plan is to obtain input and agreement from clients directly that your plan covers what is of most interest to them, and that you have captured the types of topics that came up in the relationship feedback audit and need assessment. If clients feel that they have helped you to develop a joint plan for success, they will be much more invested in helping you to succeed. You need not share the section of the plan that focuses on internal efforts to expand work from the client, but everything else will likely be of interest to them. It also reminds them of how committed you are to their success and how important they are to your firm.

9. Monitor team progress and report on results

Client teams should try to meet at least monthly to report on actions taken against the plan since the prior meeting, and on any immediate threats or opportunities. You should be soliciting feedback regularly from clients; but once a year, you should schedule a meeting for a deeper dive on how well you are meeting their needs and how you have done in executing on your client plan.

Develop a set of internal metrics to measure your success. Measurable items might include:

- a summary of interactions outside of active matters, social activities, new matters originated in the same practice group, new practice groups and new offices;
- a list of client referrals to new clients and revenue generated from referrals;
- client feedback metrics from matter to matter and year to year;
- pricing and profitability trends; and
- the percentage of the client's legal spend that goes to the firm.

Prepare a year-end report for the broader team and for management; and if warranted, celebrate successes.

Anecdotally, one firm that wanted to incentivise team collaboration and the commitment of time that lawyers spent working on client teams set aside a proportionate amount of revenue that the client had historically generated for the firm. If the team met its stated, specific and measurable objectives – including financial metrics – the entire team received the bonus to split up equally. In some larger firms, these bonuses can range from $20,000 to $100,000 for teams to divvy up among their members.

A successful key client team model: the Client Alliance Program at Morgan Lewis

Morgan Lewis – a global law firm of over 2,000 lawyers with offices across North America, Asia, Europe and the Middle East – began its Client Alliance Program (CAP) around 2005. As the firm grew larger and added more lawyers and more offices, it needed a more formal way to help those working for clients to stay coordinated and collaborative across practices and offices. Morgan Lewis has always put a premium on its 'one firm, one vision' approach and culture, and CAP teams enhance its ability to provide consistency[13] of experience, service and quality no matter whom the client is engaged with at the firm.

The CAP is overseen by Amanda Bruno, the firm's chief business development officer. CAP teams for the most part consist of between six and 15 team members, and currently comprise timekeepers who do the most work for the client across offices and practices, together with a dedicated business development manager with the relevant business and industry background. There are currently 38 active CAP teams, and Amanda believes that keeping the number of teams small (under 40) is crucial to the programme's success. Amanda kicks off each new fiscal year with training for all CAP team leaders to share expectations, metrics and a template for client action plans.

At the end of each fiscal year, the teams are reviewed quantitatively and qualitatively, and Amanda meets with all of the CAP team leaders to review the previous fiscal year's performance. "We measure success based on metrics and other goals that are stipulated in their annual client action plans," says Amanda. "Every client plan is different and is based on what we've heard from clients or know from our work with them are important priorities for us to focus on." For example, many clients have made diversity a core priority; and in addition to what the firm is already doing in this area, each CAP team adds specific action items and associated metrics to its client action plan in order to help meet or exceed the client's goals for diversity.

When asked whether the teams change from year to year, Amanda says: "Most definitely they do. Some teams begin functioning so well independently that we 'graduate' them out of the programme, so we can make room for another team. Those teams that perform the best are those whose leaders are enthusiastic and invested and make the CAP team a top priority." Unsurprisingly, the CAP teams that don't do as well are those in which CAP team leaders do not take the time to make the programme a priority. In these cases, a co-leader may be added or the CAP team will be eased out of the programme.

The programme continues to be a great success and a priority for the firm. Amanda's team measures all of the metrics of each CAP team in the 12 months before it becomes a CAP team and for the 12 months thereafter; on average, client accounts have grown by 15.5%. Amanda believes that about 50% of a CAP team's goals focus on service and relationship priorities, and 50% on expansion opportunities: "The expansion opportunities fall naturally out of the more consistent dialogue we are having with clients about their pain points and helping them look around the corner."

The firm also has a formal client feedback programme and all CAP teams are included in that process. This feedback is turned over to the CAP team leaders and incorporated into annual plans and interim strategies.

VI. SUCCESSION PLANNING – RETAINING CLIENTS OVER THE LONG TERM

1. Introduction

Transitioning or turning over clients is one of the most challenging hurdles in retirement planning, both for senior partners and for their firms. Clients know and often worry that senior partners may be nearing retirement; but in the absence of any proactive outreach by firms or senior partners about future transitions, they may make assumptions and start transitioning work to other firms.

The firms that are most successful in institutionalising clients are those in which succession is less of an issue because numerous capable lawyers have been introduced to clients throughout the lifetime of the relationship. In these firms, no client relies on a single partner. In many firms, however, compensation models encourage top partners to retain control of client relationships and, in some instances, prevent other partners from freely contacting or entertaining 'their' clients.

Firms would benefit from well-thought-out executive approaches to succession planning, so that they are prepared when lawyers begin to scale back their practices – either to make time for other pursuits or to prepare for eventual retirement. The goal is to ensure that both clients and the firm are well served during and at the conclusion of the transition period. The sooner that senior partners start thinking about their plans for retiring from the firm, the more seamless it will feel to clients and the better prepared the firm will be. Usually, planning for transition should begin at least three to five years prior to an anticipated retirement; but it is even better if senior partners with a loyal client following begin even sooner to identify who they will mentor into their practice and relationships.

There are a number of steps that firms and senior lawyers can and should take to ensure smooth client transitions, which will hopefully result in the retention of clients long after the original client relationship partners retire.

2. Assess current clients and relationships of senior partners

Do a three to five-year trend analysis of the firm's top 80% of client revenue broken down by service specialty. (This exercise is important to do at all times, not just for succession purposes, since it helps firms to assess how broadly the firm is cross-servicing/cross-selling clients.) Analyse the data to see which partners, practices and offices have been engaged with clients, and then develop a relationship map for each client that includes key members of the client's team matched to the firm's partners and associates. Don't forget that GCs and other

"The sooner that senior partners start thinking about their plans for retiring from the firm, the more seamless it will feel to clients and the better prepared the firm will be."

decision makers may also be nearing retirement or transitions, so include them in your analysis. For all clients, identify the ages of key contacts at the client as well as at the firm, to identify who is in need of relationship focus or succession.

3. Devise specific steps for transitioning each senior partner client

It is best to develop a plan for each client well in advance of the time that a senior partner will actually leave the firm, preferably looking as many as three to five years in advance. The timeframe will depend partly on the following:

- how longstanding the relationship has been;
- how well dispersed the client relationships are with others in the firm;
- the depth and breadth of services for which the client has used the firm in the past; and
- the degree to which the firm has been involved with the client over time.

The more involved that the firm and client have been, the more likely that the client will be loyal and, consequently, the easier the transition is likely to be.

Crucial to the process is identifying appropriate lawyers both to manage the relationship and to do the work for each client going forward. It is not unusual for the 'new team' to have a partner with the ability to nurture the relationship and an area of expertise specific to the client, but also to have additional lawyers on the team to provide other areas of expertise. The key is to be thoughtful when formulating the new team, choosing personalities, experience and skills that match well with particular clients and their needs. Meet with your clients to introduce all members of the team, asking for their input to make sure there are no 'mismatches'. Make clients aware of your efforts to continue to meet their needs and the firm's desire to keep serving them in the coming years. If you begin to implement your plan several years in advance, you will have the opportunity to check in with clients a few times a year to evaluate how well the transition plan is working and to make adjustments as needed.

4. Client successors

Too often, a partner has retained such close control over a client relationship that once retirement nears, there is no one in the next generation who is a good fit to become the successor. In fact, in a number of firms, there is a dearth of middle-generation partners, because those who were coming up hit a ceiling, did not get access to relationships and left their firms. Again, ideally, client successors should be identified five to 10 years before a partner retires, but certainly no later than three years. In some instances, two partners will have to serve as successors – one who is more of a trusted adviser and another who might be a top subject-matter expert in the client's industry. Whereas traditional rainmakers used to play the dual role of general trusted adviser and practice specialist, it is rare to find this today in a single partner. In some instances, firms must hire laterally for a successor.

5. Gather information about the client

There are a number of steps that firms will want to take when transitioning a client relationship from one partner to the next (again, this part of the process is something that firms should be doing with all key clients, whether or not the relationship partner is nearing retirement). The first is to develop a central repository on each client served by partners who may transition within three to five years. This will include gathering important information about the client and the firm's relationship with the client, such as:

- financial data and background information on the history of the client, to assess trends, services utilised and the evolution of the relationship over time;
- a relationship matrix that identifies and matches lawyers' relationships with different members of the client organisation;

- the firm's history of being on a preferred panel and for what services;
- the client's organisational chart;
- the client's panel of law firms and procurement policies;
- the client's annual plan;
- annual regulatory agency-required reports for public companies;
- a competitive intelligence report, litigation and deals summaries; and
- market research on client industry and competitors.

The relationship partner and the successor, as well as others in the firm who serve the client, should meet to review the information, discuss any concerns or obstacles, and identify specific issues to raise with the client. This should be converted into a client succession plan, including timelines.

6. Engage with the client about the succession plan
Once the successor(s) has been identified and the internal team has met to discuss the client (even if the team is just the current relationship partner and the successor), the relationship partner should meet in person with the client to discuss his or her plans and the proposed successor. Shortly thereafter, the successor should be introduced to the client decision maker as well as others at the client who interact with the law firm. Ideally, the client will already have met and worked with the chosen successor, and will have a familiarity and comfort level with the partner, but this is not always the case. Asking the client for input on the successor selection is critical.

7. Gauge and enhance the successor's progress
The senior partner and the successor should devise and implement a plan for the gradual transition of the relationship. This will include having the successor begin scheduling and leading meetings, sending the bills and soliciting feedback on the firm's servicing of the client. The managing partner should also meet with the client several times during the two to three-year transition period to gauge how well the transition is going, so that any issues or concerns can be addressed. This is a critical phase of the transition, as the client may be assessing whether this is the time to make a change in outside law firms. It is best to encourage open and honest dialogue in order to make any course corrections necessary, which in some cases might even include changing the successor. If the client is generally happy with the choice and how things are going, the successor should accelerate efforts to deepen the relationship, loyalty and value enhancement. Successors often benefit from some coaching from the relationship partner, another partner who is expert at client development and/or the business development professional in the firm.

8. Monitor the transition of client responsibility
Once a formal succession process has been put in place, firm management (either the managing partner or the department/practice group leader, along with the firm's CFO) should begin to assess actual transition metrics. This can be accomplished by meeting with the successor to gauge actual transition and reviewing metrics such as working hours on client files by successor, transfer of origination or billing/matter credit. Since succession planning can be challenging for senior partners and firms alike, any successes in specific succession transitions should be communicated, recognised and rewarded. One firm has added a column to its online individual partner reports dedicated to transition metrics. It indicates the hours/billings that a senior partner has transitioned to a successor. In this scenario, the compensation system rewards both partners: the partner doing the transitioning/transfer and the successor.

Each of the steps discussed here reinforces the need to begin the planning process early. All senior lawyers should think ahead to the legacy they hope to leave, and all firms must encourage these valuable individuals to share their relationships, talents and insights long before they actually leave the firm. Transitioning relationships and skillsets takes time; and for many senior lawyers and their clients, it represents a time of mixed emotions. Planning ahead carefully and thoughtfully allows the firm to develop and promote appropriate talent from within, identify laterals it may need to add, or at least be able to plan for replacing revenue and relationships that may disappear when a senior partner does depart – be it to retire full time or to pursue one of many alternate paths later in life.

Part 5. Earning loyalty through value, innovation and collaboration

I. ADDING VALUE FOR CLIENTS

1. Introduction

For at least two decades, law firms that wanted to stand out to their most important clients have provided 'added value' by giving them services for free, including CLE training and other resources that they used to charge clients for. After the global financial crisis of 2008 and the launch of the ACC Value Challenge, clients began more actively to ask for and expect value over and above the legal services they paid for. In fact, many began soliciting specific value-added services that they could expect to receive in the RFPs they issued to their outside firms.

What has not changed is that although legal departments have grown dramatically in the last 20 years, in-house lawyers continue to be spread thinly, often operating in reactive or crisis mode to get deadlines met and deliverables delivered. Clients have increasingly depended on their outside firms to provide value to them over and above the billable work they are asked to do.

Relationship and matter oversight partners should track the time and expense that their firms give to clients for these value enhancements, and discuss the findings at an annual relationship review.

This is a way for firms:

- to remind clients of the depth of their investment in the client relationship;
- to get feedback on what was worthwhile or not; and
- to start a conversation about client needs and interests in additional or alternative value services or paid services.

As with anything you do for clients, the best way to determine how best you can add value is to ask. Initiate a meaningful dialogue with each client to ask them what they most need; what you have done in the past that was or was not worthwhile; what they are receiving from other providers; and what you could do that others aren't.

2. Client relationship management and oversight
For many of their largest clients (ie, usually the top revenue-generating, repeat clients), firms will often devote as many as 100 to 200 partner hours per year that are not billed to the client. These efforts often are made regardless of whether the client has a designated, formal client team at the firm (see Part 4, Chapter V). These hours are used on initiatives such as:

- strategic conversations with the client about their business;
- short questions that clients have that firms don't 'nickel and dime' for;
- internal client team discussions and meetings on client needs, strategies and industry;
- matter budgeting;
- scoping and monitoring;
- social and entertainment activities;
- discussions with the client about ongoing matters;
- feedback and continuous improvement activities;
- discussions to resolve billing and conflict challenges; and
- panel firm conferences.

In some instances, firms even dedicate full-time relationship managers, billing managers and project managers to specific clients at no 'additional' charge to the client. These non-billable services are often provided to many clients in firms, not just the top 20, but not usually in such high volume.

3. CLE training – on-site, webinars and digital modules
As travel and expense budgets have been slashed, in-house lawyers may struggle to meet their jurisdiction's mandatory CLE requirements. In addition, legal departments often prefer their own 'bespoke' training sessions on emerging trends and new issues. Law firms often have a CLE professional on staff to obtain the necessary approvals in each

state and usually offer a range of on-site workshops, training seminars and webinars to clients on topics they are most interested in. This benefits the client, but also provides the firm with an opportunity to introduce new lawyers with different areas of expertise into the client relationship.

4. Non-legal executive, company and support training

Many of the issues that in-house lawyers work on emanate from the business itself – from the C-suite, the business units, the operations staff and the board, among others. Most of these legal issues have relevance for the business's stakeholders and could even be improved upon or avoided if some process mapping and avoidance strategies were put in place. Law firms can add great value by offering free or discounted workshops and training on topics such as:

- internal culture related to bias, harassment and discrimination;
- global compliance and risk on privacy, cybersecurity, marketing and sales practices, contracts, and legislation such as the US Foreign Corrupt Practices Act and False Claims Act; and
- crisis and risk management.

5. Collaboration among legal operations professionals

Legal departments and law firms each have grown their in-house staffs of legal operations professionals – those who support the functions of technology (tools, AI, automation), pricing, knowledge management, process and project management, vendor and law firm panel management, outsourcing and so on. It would improve both the law firm/client relationship and skills and collaboration to conduct and share training, resources and even access to shared platforms or tools.

6. Audits/policy reviews

Often as a way to evaluate whether a client could use a new service that the firm feels might be helpful, and that it could perhaps provide better than a current provider, law firms sometimes offer to conduct a limited audit of policies, training materials, employee manuals, specific types of contracts, new compliance language in documents and so on. While the scope of this value offering must be clearly defined, so that the firm does not take on an unreasonable amount for free, this is an excellent way to provide value and to demonstrate your ability to improve on what the firm might currently be doing or providing.

7. Secondments

Legal departments have long used secondments – requesting lawyers from their law firms to join the in-house legal team for a specified period – to fill a temporary need left by a lawyer on maternity/paternity or other leave, or to provide support on a large, but short-term, project basis. While some clients have required that their law

Technology solutions need to bring together people, process and technology. You can have the technology, but it has to be part of a process that is accessible, and you need the people to be convinced to use it. Getting people to change the way they do things is very hard. It has to be fast and intuitive, and show an immediate benefit.

Mark Chandler
Executive vice president, chief legal officer and chief compliance officer, Cisco Systems, Inc

firms second an associate to them for free as part of the engagement agreement, most agree to pay the associate's salary on a lower-cost basis. As law firms continue to expand their own workforces with different types of skills, levels and professional roles, clients could benefit from having others serve in seconded roles for specified rotation terms. The firm benefits from the closer ties it develops with the client and the knowledge that each secondee gains of the people, culture, approaches and philosophy of the client.

8. 'Looking around the corner' briefings and alerts

Some of the best value that lawyers can bring to in-house clients are periodic updates on new developments or trends that may affect individual clients. While digital client alerts are helpful, in-house counsel are inundated with these emails, most of which don't include a cover note that identifies issues of particular importance to the specific company/client. A better approach may be to pick up the phone for a quick call. However you do it – whether by phone, email, alerts or on-site briefings – keep clients apprised of issues that will affect them in the future.

9. Diversity

Companies are putting more pressure on outside vendors to demonstrate their commitment to diversity. Many general counsel are evaluating outside firms for their efforts and success at hiring, advancing and crediting diverse lawyers. But legal departments also struggle with improving the diversity of their teams. Law firms can add value by conducting joint recruiting efforts in which new lawyers rotate through both the client and the law firm; participate in more formal programmes, such as the Mansfield Rule programmes offered by Diversity Lab[14]; and include clients' diverse lawyers in any training that their firm provides for diverse lawyers. See Part 5, Chapter VI for more on this issue.

10. *Pro bono*

Many legal departments have no formal process to encourage and/or reward their lawyers to participate in *pro bono* activities. As most law firms do have a formal programme, often with a *pro bono* coordinator, clients can be invited to collaborate with firm lawyers on *pro bono* projects and to join them in other charitable or civic causes. Working together on charitable activities promotes collaboration, shared values and deeper, multi-dimensional relationships between clients and their firms.

II. INITIATING INNOVATION AND ALIGNING VALUE

1. Introduction

With so much talk about the need for innovation in the legal profession, many mistakenly believe that innovation in law firms is all about technology; but it is not. Some of the most fundamental innovation that is occurring has to do with how work is done, why, by whom and for whom. Innovation focuses on people, process and platform. Technology is an essential enabler of the transformation taking place in the profession; but it is not in and of itself innovation in the delivery of legal services.

Innovation must solve a problem and create value or benefit to the client business. It also addresses the critical question of who delivers legal services. Traditionally, law has been practised strictly by lawyers in law firms (and more recently by in-house lawyers in companies). Even with the recent advent of technology tools used for e-discovery, contract management and other matters, the majority of legal services provided to clients by law firms are still managed and executed by lawyers, who charge very expensive hourly rates.

No matter what your practice or the location of your market, it is time to take a look at your business model to ensure that what you do and how you do it provides the best results for the best value to your clients. Not all legal services are equally important or equally valuable to clients, so you must first get a clear idea of the specific value that your clients attach to your services. Even within your practice area, some services will be worth much more to the client than others and certain outcomes more important or worth a risk than others. No two clients will evaluate this in the same way or affix the same value or price to services.

At the outset of every new client engagement or every new matter, you need to ask each client how they define the value of the various services that you provide to them. Questions to ask include the following:

- What are they willing to pay top dollar for?
- What are the agreed-upon outcomes that they hope to achieve and the expectations for what these should cost?
- What do they perceive to be more routine work that should be charged at a lower price, delegated to an alternative legal professional or outsourced to a legal research or contract law service provider in the same jurisdiction or elsewhere?
- What matters pose the greatest risk to their own internal clients (ie, the chief executive, the board and/or the shareholders)?
- How they will measure success?

We need to balance rate reduction and innovation. Focusing entirely on rates erodes relationships with outside firms, and that cannot be the only consideration. While needing reasonable rates, I also am looking for value, expertise, efficiency and standardisation. If a firm helps us to automate and become more efficient, it may worry about losing billable hours, as we can then do these things ourselves. But in fact, it actually earns greater loyalty by producing innovative work, and I will go back to it with other, sometimes higher-value, projects.

David Mack
Senior vice president and chief legal officer, Hartford HealthCare

We ultimately had a difficult discussion with one of our outside counsel who has deep knowledge of our company and strong subject-matter expertise. When it became clear that we were going to try a new direction on a certain segment of high-volume work, we gave her and her firm the option of developing an approach to that work that used technology and alternative staffing and was much more cost effective. The partner declined, saying that her firm couldn't match the pricing and wasn't capable of investing in a new, more automated approach. While we still consult with her on some one-off, high-level issues, we don't use her or her firm the way we used to.

Associate general counsel, large US franchisor

- How will they evaluate whether a matter is worth the money required to litigate or settle?

It is critical to have candid ongoing conversations with clients about expectations, service satisfaction and, whenever possible, metrics that can demonstrate a return on investment for the client. Remember that clients are not in business to pay their lawyers or to help them meet their firm's billable hour and origination quotas. They are in business to help manage risk, increase sales and profits, and build sustainable, successful companies. Lawyers are a cost of doing business and represent a significant expense to many companies – hence the increased scrutiny on cost and efficiency. Clients don't want to bear the brunt of lawyers and firms that do not operate efficiently, and they also want and need their own costs to be predictable.

An associate general counsel of a large franchisor shared a relatively common story about a lawyer/firm she inherited early on in her role:

> *When I first started at the company, I inherited a partner from a law firm that had been doing work for a now retired division counsel for decades. He billed us less by the hour than other law firms and on its face, it appeared that he delivered better value to the company. But it was a false narrative and he ultimately was more expensive because of the number of hours associated with the work. Once we took a data-driven approach to understanding the total spend, it became clear that the reason the prior lawyer was billing us for so many hours, albeit at a lower hourly rate, is because he wasn't doing a good job of addressing the issues at the outset of the contract negotiation, which ultimately led to a lot of work on the back end amending the contracts and sometimes resulting in agreements being terminated. While the former division counsel was upset and felt badly that this lawyer had given his 'life's blood' to our company, the business case was clear. It wasn't intended as a personal judgement or slight; but the best interest for the company was to go in another direction.*

2. Innovation: how to enable and align value with clients

Innovation is the hottest topic in the legal profession right now, followed closely by legal operations. Clients seem to want or demand it; new competitors are aggressively disrupting; and law firms are trying to innovate. Despite or perhaps because of all the hype, there is a fair amount of scepticism, confusion and trepidation about what it means and how to execute innovation in the law firm setting. Some firms that are innovating are doing so in a vacuum, without collaborating directly with clients.

Even in firms that have hired innovation officers, pricing specialists and project managers, and developed technology solutions and lower-cost legal service centres, busy partners often don't have the time or know-how to advance these concepts and conversations directly with their clients. Unfortunately, many partners in firms (and also senior in-house lawyers) still resist change, and are not aware of or comfortable with the many ways that their firms can and should be aggressively pursuing alternative and innovative processes to both create and deliver value to clients.

An excellent resource for in-house counsel and law firms is a white paper published by the ACC called *Unless You Ask: A Guide for Law Departments to Get More from External Relationships*.[15] We will discuss four of the fundamental components of delivering value to clients:

- knowledge management;
- process and project management;
- data analytics; and
- scoping, staffing, budgeting and billing.

When selecting a lawyer or firm, clients are looking for subject-matter expertise and creativity in solving legal problems. Now there is a growing focus on innovative service delivery and creativity in how the legal work is done. Usually, this selection process is driven by legal operations teams within the legal department (if one exists); but the decision still lies with the in-house attorneys.

Lucy Endel Bassli
Former assistant general counsel for legal operations at Microsoft; now founder and innovation coach, trainer and consultant at InnoLaw Group

3. Implementing knowledge management

Knowledge management in law firms is derived by creating systems, platforms and processes to capture knowledge assets, expertise, experience and prior work product. If effective, knowledge management enables firms to capture and collect, store, share and refine knowledge that provides value to clients and the firm. It prevents firms from reinventing the wheel and avoids the common problem of different lawyers in the firm using their own forms or pricing models or cutting and pasting from prior documents, which creates inconsistency, uneven quality and inefficiency.

In order to develop an effective knowledge management system, firms should never begin research from scratch, but should rather check with lawyers, the librarian or knowledge specialist, the firm intranet and other central sources to see where other precedents, forms and memos can be found to build from, and establish their own knowledge repositories. If your firm is large enough, hire a knowledge management professional to direct and oversee the design process, technology platform and ongoing management of knowledge. Define knowledge management goals on the purposes for which and how knowledge will be used; and then determine the type of information to be gathered and stored, and where that information will be found (you may want to include client preferences in this assessment).

Once you have developed your knowledge platform, you have to decide how that knowledge will be accessed, by whom and when, including those in the firm as well as clients. It is critical to success that your firm's culture supports knowledge creation, new knowledge development, education and collaboration. You will need methods to continuously track and assess current and future knowledge needs, keep knowledge current and cull outdated information and forms. Clients will want to know:

- how attorneys utilise the firm's knowledge management;
- how they can access the firm's knowledge management;
- how much time and how many lawyers and others devote to building knowledge repositories; and
- how clients benefit from this resource and strategy.

Clients will increasingly want to see your metrics on this.

4. Implementing process and project management
The role of project management is to ensure that cases, matters and transactions are completed using:

- the right staffing in terms of skills, level and cost;
- processes and timelines to map and monitor workflow against schedules; and
- objectives/outcomes and budgets that are developed and met, all while still achieving desired outcomes or results.

We find that firms say they have project managers, data analysts and good technology, but they aren't actually using these resources effectively. In fact, many of the professionals doing this work are expensive lawyers, not dedicated experts, and they aren't using data to help predict cases and outcomes.

Associate general counsel, multinational company

Many law firms now often utilise project management software and technology; employ certified and experienced project managers; and train their lawyers to work beside these resources to better manage client work and expectations.

There is a beginning and end to each project or matter. Effective project management helps projects to stay on track, in scope and within budget. In the law firm context, the components typically involved in project management include:

- scoping matters, case assessment, establishing goals and outcomes;
- process mapping, assigning tasks and timelines;
- effective management of and communications with and across the team;
- planning and managing a detailed budget;
- assessing and assigning risk; and
- monitoring scope, quality, budget and outcomes, and negotiating change orders.

Business process improvement is a systematic approach to help an organisation to optimise its underlying processes to achieve more efficient results. Process improvement is also a method to introduce process changes to improve the quality of a product or service, to better match customer needs. The Lean Six Sigma[16] framework called DMAIC is often used as a tool to engage in continuous improvement:

- **D**efine the problem/client need and why it needs to be solved.
- **M**easure the process's current performance using a process map and baseline measures.
- **A**nalyse the root causes of and opportunities to reduce waste or consider variations.
- **I**mprove the process by designing, testing, implementing and validating changes to the process.
- **C**ontrol the process to ensure that changes to the process 'stick' – that is, that they are permanent and sustainable.

While there is still pushback from lawyers who believe that they cannot predict the path that a case will take (this is especially true for litigators) or cannot estimate budgets, clients will no longer accept these objections. Most work plans allow for out-of-scope modification and 'work change orders' if the client and the lawyer agree that a different or additional workflow is needed once entrenched in the matter.

Legal work needs to be disaggregated so that the right resource is used at the right level and price. Aside from the need for diversity, we don't really care how our law firms decide to resource matters to achieve the results we need if they can provide a competitive price or a creative, value-based approach to fees. That said, we typically won't agree these days to pay associate rates for document review.

Head of legal operations, Fortune 100 company

In order to develop an effective process and project management system, firms should:

- interview clients to assess their current usage of and views on project management tools, platforms and successful application;
- assess their own technology tools and platforms to determine whether and what new resources will be required;
- analyse project management support roles required for each practice area and hire accordingly;
- train lawyers on tools and to work alongside project management professionals on current/new matters;
- develop rigorous monitoring, reporting and feedback mechanisms;
- be prepared to provide clients with tools, approaches and metrics regarding project management, as well as dedicated personnel and their training/certification; and
- provide clients with examples of process maps that the firm has used for them.

5. Implementing better scoping, staffing, budgeting and billing practices

An essential component of effective project management is the development of a proper scoping plan right at the outset of an engagement. It is critical to clarify the project goals and scope, to ensure that the engagement does not experience too much scope creep or, worse, go off the rails. Discuss with clients how their budget might affect the approaches you take, the options they will have and possible outcomes. Doing so may prevent you from spending a lot of time on a project that the client does not expect or want to be charged for, or going down a road that the client doesn't believe is important relative to the cost or risk.

I am not interested in telling law firms how to run their business, but I am very clear on who at the firm is most valuable to us. Sometimes the people most valuable don't get the recognition or credit inside the firm they deserve, and I provide input to management on who is valuable and why. In recent years, I actually have changed the engagement letter we use to add a 'key person' clause which allows me to invoke an early termination of the agreement if 60% or more of the key people on a team leave the firm.

Associate general counsel, large franchisor

5.1 Scoping

During a kick-off meeting of the client and the outside lawyers, a plan should be developed that addresses and documents the following:

- the background on the matter;
- a general and detailed (broken down by task) description of the project;
- what a successful/the desired outcome will look like;
- the deliverables;
- the goals and metrics that will be used to measure progress and success;
- the client's expectations for the engagement, as well as the assumptions, risks, unknowns and potential roadblocks;
- early case assessment, if a litigation matter;
- the scope of legal work to be performed;
- staffing;
- the steps and phases of work and the person responsible for each;
- a timeline to completion, with milestones and critical benchmarks; and
- a system to monitor and report on progress.

5.2 Staffing

Once the project is well defined, the next step is to determine how best to staff it for maximum efficiency and effectiveness. This will include consideration of expertise needed, and whether that can be provided by in-house lawyers and paralegals, outside law firms, ALSPs, experts and other outsourcing options. In addition to lawyers, many other professionals often can or should be considered to support the execution of a project – consultants, patent agents, data analysts, e-discovery contractors, paralegals and so on. The ideal team will structure work being done by the least expensive resource who has the experience and skills to complete that part of each project effectively. Once the team is selected, there should be an organisational chart that breaks down roles, responsibilities and reporting structure, with an identified project leader.

5.3 Budgeting and pricing

Preparing a well-scoped project plan should make budgeting a matter easier. In many cases, budget estimates will have been developed during an RFP process or even a less formal proposal/engagement process. Initial estimates should be revisited and revised once the preliminary scoping meeting has occurred, to ensure more thorough assessment of staffing, timelines, other expenses (eg, e-discovery, experts, travel) and scope. This then becomes the project budget.

If flat or capped fees have been agreed, it is critical for the law firm team to develop systems to manage against the budget and to monitor in real time the actual time and costs against the budget. If the fee is a finite fixed fee with no ability to 'true up', firms will have to focus on leverage and delegation to make work profitable. Out-of-scope requests or deviations should be addressed early and often, to avoid budget overruns or any billing surprises.

A budget for any legal matter can be easily set up and managed using readily available spreadsheet software such as Microsoft Excel or an electronic billing system which incorporates a budgeting feature. The advantage of using spreadsheet software over an electronic billing system is the greater degree of flexibility in designing a budget template in a spreadsheet format that meets the needs of a particular client and a specific legal matter, while still retaining them.

The budgeting process is a critical point at which the firm and the client's operations experts should be involved: procurement and pricing experts can work effectively at the outset to establish milestones, dashboards and red flag alerts, and confirm how clients want to be notified of any possible overages.

5.4 Billing

The majority of law firms use the billable hour as their primary tracking and billing model. Fortunately, time-keeping methods and applications have improved significantly with the use of recording time in real time and passive mechanisms to track time. Clients often require their firms to use e-billing technology and outside counsel guidelines have made it much more difficult for firms to bill for time that is not well defined or allowed for in the guidelines.

Unfortunately, many lawyers are in firms that don't mandate using time tracking technology, so they often reverse engineer their time at the end of every month or week. This results in uncaptured time or inaccurate data. With so many technology tools available, clients have little tolerance for firms that do not track time in real time. This data becomes critical to the data analytics component discussed above in helping clients to predict costs going forward and also to avoid surprises in bills – clients hate surprises related to invoices.

Clients are likely to want to delve into a firm's billing practices. For

Law firms need to be much tidier with their billing records and comply with a client's billing guidelines. General counsel understandably get very irritated with firms that ignore and violate them. We assign numbers internally and when the legal department misses the numbers, the GC is called out at board meetings. They can even be fired if they don't meet their numbers. Firms must prepare accurate budgets and meet the spend goals and understand the pressure their clients are under from the CEO.

Former chief of staff and senior director of legal operations, multinational technology company

example, they may want to know what the duration is between when lawyers actually perform work versus when they record their time for that work (a delay in recording can lead to errors, lack of detail, overbilling or underbilling.) Clients will also want to know whether the firm requires timekeepers to record time in real time digitally and what tools the firm uses to do so.

As with most engagements, setting expectations and communicating effectively are critical to satisfying the needs of clients. It is essential to develop good project and scoping plans and budgets; but these are not enough. Frequent communication about the status of matters, real time spend versus estimates, any delays or other concerns or developments should be part of weekly update calls and emails with clients.

5.5 Implementing data analytics

Clients are looking to law firms to use data in ways that will help them to provide better service, value and efficiency. They are accessing publicly available data on billing rates and costs for types of matters across jurisdictions, and then combining that with their own analysis of data histories on cases, costs, firms, timelines and outcomes. Clients want firms to be able to better predict the cost and price of cases, matters and transactions at the portfolio, matter or task level.

In addition to more common use of data analytics to negotiate flat or alternative fees and prepare budgets, clients and firms are using data to help with predictive analytics on outcomes of cases, verdicts and the amount of time that a case is likely to take. However, clients are frustrated with how long it is taking law firms to embrace the use of data.

In order to implement disciplined and effective data tools and utilisation, law firms should:

- define the goals of collecting and analysing data – for example, analysis of costs and profitability, development of alternative fee arrangements, staffing, budgets to actual, staffing scenarios and impact on pricing;
- determine the tools and types of data that they currently have available and identify additional data that is needed, as well as tools to monitor and flag data points;
- find out where data currently resides in the firm and who else can be partnered with to retrieve and analyse data – for example, the HR, IT, finance and billing departments;
- assess the quality of the data and how it is received, including format, accuracy and accessibility;
- talk to clients to ensure that the firm and its clients are tracking

similar data, and to understand what the client is doing with the data and how it is using metrics to measure its own costs as well as the performance of its law firms;
- use the right technology and process/project management (see above) to collect data and evaluate the data to measure metrics and manage for better efficiency and outcomes;
- train their lawyers in how to use data for their matters, pricing, scoping, risk assessments and outcome scenarios, and how to communicate about data/metrics with clients;
- be prepared to talk to clients about what types of data they track and find out what data would be most helpful to the client for them to collect and report on; and
- describe specific examples of how they have used data analytics for other clients and explore ways that they could expand similar usage for this client.

One of the most important things that your firm can do with respect to innovation is to engage proactively in thoughtful conversations with clients. How do they use technology? Data analytics? What are their biggest challenges in trying to be more efficient and reduce their outside legal spend? What do you or they do currently that is inefficient or poses risks to the company?

Always explore ways to use technology to your client's advantage. Find out what software your clients use and try to use the same software for your reports and case management. Look for technology tools and uses that can streamline project management, litigation management, case assessment and task estimating. Use Extranets and shareware for larger clients, to facilitate document and information sharing. Stay current on new technology tools and resources that could make you more efficient and more accurate.

Finally, consider whether outsourcing options might be more efficient and effective for certain types of work. Many clients and firms now outsource legal research, contract management and other routine work to contract lawyers at home or overseas. Talk to clients about whether they do this now and how it is working. Look at your own firm to see whether there are more cost-effective ways to get administrative and even legal research work done, and show clients how you are passing those savings on to them.

Exelon has a core firm programme and for the most part our loyalty as a company is with those firms, which means that we invest in those relationships and give those an opportunity to be considered for all new work. That relationship and their loyalty are earned over time and with a proven track record. The criteria we established to consider who merits a position as a core firm include the following:

- *They provide a quality work product and results;*
- *They reflect our values;*
- *They are committed to our business; and*
- *They use rates that reflect the market price.*

With these firms, we invest our time, introduce them to more people in our company and give them opportunities to get more work from us.

Melissa Lauderdale-Ward
Chief of staff to Thomas O'Neill, senior vice president and general counsel, Exelon

III. CLIENT CONVERGENCE AND PREFERRED PROVIDER PANELS

1. Introduction

Companies continue to reduce the number of outside law firms that they work with through convergence processes that result in preferred law firm panels or networks. This initiative is intended to:

- reduce the administrative burden of managing scores or hundreds of individual firms;
- reduce costs through volume discounts and flat fees;
- enhance quality, consistency and efficiency through scale; and
- build stronger and trusting partnerships with fewer law firms which are invested in the company.

Unfortunately, convergence efforts have not been as effective as intended for many legal departments or their law firms. There are a number of reasons for this. First, the design and set-up of the convergence process are not always well researched and structured. The in-house department can claim to have undertaken the process; but if it wasn't well thought out, it often falls short of its objectives. Second, very often, once a company concludes the selection of its panel firms, post-convergence management falls short. More effort has gone into the RFP and selection process than the implementation. And third, many in-house lawyers resist following panel guidelines of only using the newly selected firms. The good news for incumbent firms is that they often retain work due to their loyal relationships with inside counsel. The bad news is that newly selected firms to the panel often find that they are receiving little, if any new work from the client as far as two or three years down the road.

Perhaps one of the best-known convergence initiatives, DuPont was one of the first large companies to design and execute a convergence process in the 1990s. Over a three-year period, the company reduced its outside counsel firms from 350 to 34. It developed the DuPont Legal Model, which was a guide to how its firms would follow its expectations concerning alternative fees, strategic partnering, diversity and the use of new technologies and knowledge management. To demonstrate its commitment to its panel firms, DuPont ran annual conferences, paid for advertising of its individual firms in legal trade publications and initiated an annual diversity award programme.

According to the associate general counsel of a large franchisor:

> *When we first did our convergence process in 2016, we sent out a lot of RFPs for every new matter or chunk of work. We got tired of doing them and firms that weren't selected got tired of responding*

to them. Instead, we now are partnering with our preferred provider firms and looking to build stronger relationships and mutual value. Three of our firms have invested significant time and resources getting to know our business and building automation tools and using alternative staffing to do larger volumes of work, which has resulted in significant cost savings. In these instances, the firms have not only earned our loyalty, but also the opportunity to bid on additional work that could similarly be done more efficiently. Our firms build value and loyalty by investing in technology and process mapping in return for a greater volume of our work.

A different approach to RFPs was shared by another associate general counsel of a multinational: "We are using RFPs more within our preferred panel. The reason is that it helps us get more than one perspective. We don't always go with the cheapest firm and more often go with a firm that provides strategy and a targeted and commercial approach. This gives our firms, and in particular non-incumbent firms, an opportunity to show off their expertise."

Vincent Cordo, former central legal operations officer at Shell, suggested that responding to RFPs on the PERSUIT RFP platform,[17] which is now used by many in-house departments, is a good way for panel firms to be considered and adjust their pricing in real time. According to Jim Delkousis, the founder of software as a service (SaaS) company PERSUIT, the main advantage for in-house departments is that they can issue and evaluate RFPs to their panel firms in real time, with more consistency and transparency, and in an easy-to-compare, digestible format. Assuming that the client inputs the right questions, it can evaluate:

- a firm's proposed strategy;
- how it would run the case;
- where its weaknesses would be;
- how it would staff the project; and
- what the fee would be.

(In Part 5, Chapter VI, we will address the advantages of the staffing component as a way to seek diversity and inclusion (D&I) metrics and commitments.)

We just finished the third renewal of our preferred counsel network (PCN). We do this evaluation and renewal every three years. Over 50% of our panel firms remain in the PCN, which is a sign that it is working well; and in recent years, PCN firms received close to 90% of the outside firm legal spend.

Maureen Harms
Associate general counsel and managing counsel, 3M Co

2. Steps to make preferred panel networks a good investment for your firm

2.1 Be selective – evaluate whether a specific client panel is right for your firm

Determine how it is structured, how it is managed and what the client's objectives are. For example, is it primarily to get discounts or to

We have a very strong sourcing (procurement) group that partners with us to retain the best firm in each situation. When procurement first came on the scene, we understood that it couldn't just be about price, because if we just drove it towards the cheapest provider there would be misalignment. We found when we did that, the firms gave us the B team instead of the A team, so we'd fire them, making us both unhappy. The person who manages legal procurement is a lawyer, so she gets it, and is a business-minded person. While the focus is not on the relationships per se, *she works with us and our law firms to negotiate mutually agreeable terms and build relationships.*

Associate general counsel, multinational technology company

be more effective in firm oversight and coordination by reducing the number of outside firms? If the client has already been using a preferred provider panel model, determine what percentage of its legal work is going to new firms on the panel versus incumbent firms. Also, evaluate the number and nature of other firms being considered and what your chances are of getting on the panel. What other firms is the client considering and how many firms is the client hoping to have on its panel?

2.2 Engage actively during the process

Talk to and befriend the client's key contacts on their procurement, legal, legal operations and technology teams. Have your internal resources talk to the client's team peers. You may even help them to shape their post-selection implementation so that it is more effective for the client (and for you). Establishing a dialogue between multiple stakeholders will help you to reach out to these individuals once the panel is finalised.

2.3 Invest in the client and participate proactively from day one

Don't wait for the client to invite you to a conference for its panel firms, as these usually aren't scheduled for six to 12 months after the panel has been put together. Try to initiate a discussion early on to establish key client expectations and guidelines, and gain any knowledge about the client's immediate or short-term needs and how you might help to serve them.

2.4 Be a good team player

Certain legal departments – for example, the Pfizer Legal Alliance – require panel firms to work together on matters and share knowledge and strategies. Even if inter-firm collaboration is not mandated, the client will benefit when firms work together on its behalf. And if the panel has been carefully designed, with firms designated as 'specialists' or with a specific geographic footprint, referrals often occur between panel firms.

2.5 Use this opportunity to innovate

Clients are looking for new ways to innovate. This doesn't mean having a firm come up with a new tool. It means looking for ways to change how legal services are delivered. This might be through staffing, efficiency through automation, process mapping to cut out inefficiencies, predictive modelling and so on.

2.6 Don't use the 'B' team

Too often, once selected for a panel, firms decide that in order to be profitable, since they have often promised deep discounts, they need to shift work to lower-level and/or less productive lawyers. While it is always smart to look at more efficient and leveraged staffing models, this will destroy the firm's standing with the client.

2.7 Look for opportunities to expand

Once on a panel, firms that focus on delivering exceptional service and value, and that have a well-coordinated process in place for ongoing dialogue with multiple contacts, are often tapped for additional needs that may not have been identified in the convergence RFP or selection process.

"Talk to and befriend the client's key contacts on their procurement, legal, legal operations and technology teams. Have your internal resources talk to the client's team peers. You may even help them to shape their post-selection implementation so that it is more effective for the client (and for you)."

IV. CROSS-SERVING CLIENTS (AKA CROSS-SELLING)

1. Introduction

The easiest and most cost-effective way to grow your firm's revenue is to provide multiple services to existing clients. However, this can be done only if clients are very satisfied with the services and value that you already provide to them. Satisfied clients, especially loyalists, are predisposed to view the firm's other lawyers favourably and more likely to be receptive to all the other things the firm can do for them in its range of practice capabilities. Your focus must first be on ensuring that your clients are extremely satisfied, that you are responding to their needs and that you are creating value for them.

I personally don't think cross-selling is very effective. When I want to know who to hire for an ancillary matter or a completely different matter and I'm talking to someone who I trust at a big large firm, I will often ask, "Who would you recommend if your firm couldn't do the work?" I know they will normally tell me, "My partner down the hall is the best person you could hire to do this." There are economic incentives, social incentives, all kinds of incentives to do so; so you've got to discount it, and I do.

Mark Chandler
Executive vice president, chief legal officer and chief compliance officer, Cisco Systems, Inc

Cross-selling should be called 'cross-serving', because cross-selling implies and too often aptly describes what many lawyers do: try to sell their clients a new service that they may not want or need. As when trying to attract any new client to the firm, cross-selling should be done only after assessing the needs of the client, finding out how those needs are currently being met and identifying potential opportunities where you might find a fit between the client's needs and the services or expertise that someone else in the firm can offer the client to satisfy this need.

It is important to recognise that effective cross-serving requires two types of trust on the part of both partners and clients. The first is relational trust. Introducing a new person or team of people to the client may feel risky for the partner and requires some vulnerability. If the partner has developed loyalty with the client, there will inevitably be some anxiety about whether the new partners will provide the same level of service and personalised attention as he or she does to the client. There also is natural worry that other partners might 'steal' the client. The client also worries about whether the level of service and quality will be the same.

The second type of trust required is competence trust. The relationship partner wants to be certain that the partners whom he or she introduces to the client have the requisite skills and experience, and in many ways, are the best option for the client for a legal need that has emerged. From the outset, partners newly introduced to clients must provide value and proactively identify potential issues and ideas for the client, and prepare and interact productively – even in the first meeting or phone call.

2. Benefits of cross-selling

If you do have a highly satisfied client, expanding your representation of that client should benefit both you and the client. Firms finally recognise that the most effective way to build sustainable and profitable revenue is to further institutionalise clients, striving to serve as many of their needs as they can and are qualified to do.

2.1 Why law firms benefit from cross-selling

There are a number of reasons why cross-selling makes good business sense for law firms. First, it costs considerably more (often more than six times as much) in business development time and dollars to get a new client than to expand work from an existing client. Second, getting more lawyers involved in the relationship deepens and broadens loyalty to the firm, diminishing the risk that if one partner leaves, the client will follow. This can also help to smooth over rough edges if there is a service problem in a particular area. Third, very satisfied clients with multiple and deep relationships may be less likely to put law firms through the RFP process every time they need additional help or help in a new area. Fourth, representing a client across business areas enhances the firm's understanding of the client's business, needs, challenges and industry. Finally, the cost of switching firms becomes a greater deterrent for the client.

Heidi K Gardner – author of *Smart Collaboration: How Professionals and Their Firms Succeed in Breaking Down Silos*[18] and creator of the Smart Collaboration Accelerator – has conducted significant research

"The biggest impediment to collaboration and cross-selling is compensation systems that primarily reward self-origination, that don't penalise partners for hoarding and that don't recognise partners who share contacts and efforts."

into the data behind collaborative firms. She distinguishes between cross-selling and collaboration, noting that cross-selling more often is the act of one partner in a practice area referring a new matter to a partner in a different practice area. While this is still more beneficial than a client which is only served by one partner or one practice group, firms that solve client problems in a multi-disciplinary way across multi-practices and offices actually achieve much greater profitability and long-term loyalty (see more on collaboration in Part 5, Chapter V).

2.2 Why clients benefit from cross-selling

Clients also reap rewards when they use firms in multiple practice areas. First, clients often get a better solution when lawyers with different areas of expertise consider and understand the client's business to solve problems. Second, long-term relationships enable better collaboration between the client and the firm, resulting in better efficiency and smoother workflow. Third, it is expensive for clients to engage multiple firms, so consolidating more work into fewer is cost effective. Fourth, being an important client provides opportunities to share software and billing technologies and other resources. Finally, clients know that giving a firm a bigger piece of the pie likely qualifies them for fee larger discounts and more value-added services.

Clients today ask and expect much more of their lawyers than they did decades ago. Increasingly complex regulations across global platforms, the closer relationship of the legal function to executive office/business operations, and the demand for more efficiency and effectiveness all support the argument for multi-disciplinary approaches. In addition, there are numerous specific drivers, in that clients want lawyers who:

- deeply understand their businesses and industries;
- take a pragmatic approach to problem solving;
- consider their legal options and strategies in light of business objectives and priorities; and
- are more efficient and effective through collaboration and use of institutional and collective knowledge and technology.

3. Firms need to address their internal barriers to cross-selling

There are often numerous internal barriers that prevent cross-selling from working effectively in law firms. The biggest impediment to collaboration and cross-selling is compensation systems that primarily reward self-origination, that don't penalise partners for hoarding and that don't recognise partners who share contacts and efforts. This often results in partners who are focused only on the 'pitch' – selling anything and everything to clients without any idea of whether the client wants or needs what the lawyer is pitching, in the hope of

"Unless firms are vigilant about setting up key client teams or industry groups and developing integrated service strategies on a per-client basis, many of the lawyers in different practice areas may interact only on a sporadic, limited or superficial basis, such as at an annual retreat."

landing new work for which they will be compensated. The focus is on their own personal gain, rather than what is best for or needed by the client.

Another significant impediment is that partners in mid-sized and large firms – especially those with multiple offices – often don't know enough about the firm's other capabilities, their partners' expertise and representative matters to offer these to clients. Unless firms are vigilant about setting up key client teams or industry groups and developing integrated service strategies on a per-client basis, many of the lawyers in different practice areas may interact only on a sporadic, limited or superficial basis, such as at an annual retreat. Busy lawyers often don't even take the time to brainstorm with those in their own practice groups about client needs and cross-selling opportunities.

A third challenge is that there is often a substantial risk to the referring partner that the partner introduced for a different type of expertise may not truly be the best choice for the client relative to competitors. On a related note, partners have been harmed by cross-selling if the partner introduced does a poor job, is not responsive or is arrogant. Partners have actually lost clients as a result of cross-selling. Partners may recall clients who were made unhappy, or were even lost, due to cross-selling colleagues who were unresponsive, took too long on a matter or communicated infrequently with the client. And those still building relationships often fear that introducing another lawyer to a client might dilute their own contact with the client.

Fourth, firms regularly hire and reward laterals who have their own portable client bases (who often work hard to keep control of the relationships so that they can leave at will). Many lateral partners are not interested in introducing new partners to their clients and hold them close.

As rainmakers with distinctive areas of expertise have become increasingly mobile, they have grown more inclined to build, control and protect portable client portfolios that can be taken to a new firm with lower risk of dispersed client loyalties. On the flipside, current partners in the firm might generally be willing to cross-sell, but reluctant to do so with laterals. Often, they have been burned previously by either a lateral or other partners leaving the firm and taking their client with them.

Finally, as we have discussed in other sections of this book, many lawyers have become so specialised in their field of expertise that it has become difficult for them to think strategically outside their own practice silo. Partners may do well exploring needs that the client has in other areas of the business or issues within the partner's expertise that perhaps the client hasn't thought of or may be using another firm for. These are good opportunities to expand within a practice area; however, the best rainmakers are well versed in broader business and legal issues, and comfortably raise issues and questions and listen for indicators. This does not mean that partners have to become experts in every other legal specialty – or even in business management; but they have to learn enough about the business to ask questions and explore strategies.

Likewise, clients are also frequently siloed. In-house counsel often do not communicate across practice specialties; and different administrative and operational executives responsible for related operational functions – such as finance, human resources, distribution and logistics and marketing – rarely collaborate. These silos make it challenging to cross-sell and require internal contacts and allies to build bridges. Helping clients to be more collaborative is often a value that law firms can facilitate.

4. Cross-serve effectively

4.1 Take the 'sell' out of it

Don't treat cross-selling as a way to pitch more services or lawyers to the client. Instead, be genuine in looking for client needs that you or the firm may be able to help with, and explore with them how those needs are being met by others. Don't assume that you are the best or only solution. Remember that clients usually do not want to displace current counsel. Never go to a lunch or meeting with a client who believes you are coming to find out how things are going and instead bring a lawyer with you who wants to sell a different service to the client. The focus must be on the client's needs first, not on getting more business.

4.2 Do your homework in advance

Do some research about the kinds of issues that you think the client may have or need help with. You can do this through library services, online and by talking to the client and other professionals who advise the client. Ensure that you are knowledgeable about the client's industry and have read their annual report. Find out who is helping them with other needs now and the level of satisfaction they have with their current firm. Don't try to sell the client something if they either don't have a need for it or already feel well served by another law firm.

4.3 Discuss options and explore solutions

In discussing needs with the client, be open to helping them to find a solution using their existing resources. Rather than offering them a full-blown service option that the client may not be ready for, break it down into smaller projects that you could offer as discrete, fixed-price components that won't require the client to take all work away from another law firm. In other words, go in as an expert on a small slice first; don't try to get the whole pie at once.

4.4 Understand by whom and how hiring decisions are made

As mentioned above, in-house legal departments and companies themselves often operate as separate business units or in functional siloes. Clients themselves may not be in a position to discuss broader legal needs or be in a position to introduce a partner to others. Discussing the legal department's and company's organisational chart, and how and by whom decisions are made, will help partners to devise an approach to which clients are receptive and feel they can bring value to their team or the business.

4.5 Collaborate with your partners

Use firm client team and industry group meetings to explore ways in which other partners can help you to add value to your clients or ways in which your expertise could benefit others' clients. As long as the purpose of a meeting is clear upfront, bring a relevant partner with you when trying to explore additional needs that a client may have – don't be overly possessive or protective of your relationships and be willing to 'share credit' with others partners who can help you grow the client pie.

4.6 At all times, listen to clients

Whenever you talk to clients, always ask questions about how their business is doing, new executive hires or shake-ups, trends in the industry and threats from competitors or the economy. Ask regularly for feedback on your service and the service of others now working for the client. Formal client interviews are an excellent way to explore other needs, who they use for these and whether there might be an opportunity for your firm to do some of this work instead.

4.7 Be knowledgeable about your own firm's capabilities

Review your firm's website to learn about practice niches, specialties, industries and markets represented, and office and lawyer strengths. Also become familiar with available skills inventories and case and transaction databases that your firm might keep. Know what areas of specific expertise your colleagues have and find out how their services could benefit your client. Identify the firm's strengths and areas of distinctive expertise. Provide partners in the firm with snapshots of your practice niches and services that clients might need to make it easier for them to discuss additional service requirements.

4.8 Get your foot in the door

One of the best ways to get introduced to others in the client's legal

"As long as the purpose of a meeting is clear upfront, bring a relevant partner with you when trying to explore additional needs that a client may have – don't be overly possessive or protective of your relationships and be willing to 'share credit' with others partners who can help you grow the client pie."

department who are responsible for a different practice area from that which the firm currently serves, or to introduce another partner with different capability to a client, is to identify a small project that the firm can do for free or for a reduced cost. These discrete projects should entice the client, because the issues and risks that the client faces may be due to new regulation or case law.

Examples of this might include:

- reviewing a company's policies in a specific function;
- conducting an audit or assessment of contract documents;
- reviewing the company's website;
- looking for non-compliance or areas of risk;
- holding a training workshop for company executives, board members or staff; or
- providing a benchmark assessment of where the client is *vis-à-vis* competitors and peers.

The goal is to get the chance to work with the client in a new area, understanding that it likely already has lawyers serving this need. A discrete project that showcases the firm's expertise and ability to achieve outcomes, and that reflects a superlative, client-centric service approach, can often be a great opportunity to secure an engagement for additional work in an area that the firm has not previously serviced.

4.9 Initiate discussions with decision makers on strategy

Something that clients often complain about is that they don't have enough time or energy to think strategically about their priorities and goals, and how the legal team could better meet the needs of, and add value to, the business. Partners should suggest to clients – assuming that they are in some sort of management/oversight role – that they schedule a strategic brainstorming session at no cost to the client. Partners should come prepared with knowledge about the company, the industry and the client's competitors to be well versed in exploring the kinds of issues for which the client may need solutions.

4.10 Communicate with clients about things of relevance to them

Surveys show that clients are commonly aware of only 30% of the services that a firm has to offer. Remind them of the firm's areas of expertise, specific results and 'wins', and alert them to areas of concern or change. If others in the firm author alerts or articles that may be of interest, send these to clients along with a personal note or email – but be sure that the communication they receive is tailored to their industry or type of business need.

4.11 Communicate internally about clients and opportunities

Celebrate cross-selling successes – nothing motivates behaviour as much as tangible results. Updates can be incorporated in a firm's daily internal newsletter, alert or bulletin, included as an addendum to new matter openings and presented at attorney meetings.

5. Some additional tips to improve cross-selling efforts

- Stay focused on what is best for the client: look for actual needs they have and explore with them how those needs are being met by others. Don't assume that you are the best or only solution. Remember that clients usually do not want to displace current counsel.
- Proactively look for opportunities to cross-sell, but do your homework first. Identify clients that are in industries or are of a type likely to need your area of expertise.
- Look at the firm's largest clients and analyse by practice area where fees have been billed over the past three years. Look for up and down trends and voids.
- Conduct research on possible targets. Find out who they use now for various legal services.
- Talk to and listen to your clients. Ask a lot of questions that will help you to better understand their business, industry trends, new offices or acquisitions, major initiatives or challenges, competitive and financial pressures, and so on.
- Look out for key indicators that the client may need additional legal services, such as mergers, acquisitions or divestitures; financial restructuring or a change in capital raising; new management changes and new executives; new products, business units or innovations; new offices and/or international activity; re-engineering; stock price variations; and competitor, industry or economic threats.
- Know what areas of specific expertise your colleagues have and talk to them in advance to find out how their services could benefit your client and specific questions that you should ask the client. Identify the firm's strengths and areas of distinctive expertise.
- Only try to cross-sell another lawyer or practice area if:
  - there is no question of the skill or knowledge of that person or group;
  - doing so will not be duplicative of what the client already receives effectively from another lawyer or law firm; and
  - the lawyers are committed to the client and deliver what has been promised.
- Become fully knowledgeable about the firm's resources, capabilities and administrative staff. Ensure that you know who to call for what.
- Be prepared to sell a discrete 'product' or service – for example, an assessment or audit –that will allow you to get your foot in

the door, but not force the client to fire an existing law firm.

- Provide partners in the firm with snapshots of other practice niches and services that clients might need, to make it easier for them to discuss additional service needs.
- Determine what lawyers in other firms are currently providing services to your client. Find out how satisfied the client is with these firms and how solid the relationships are. Ask how they select law firms in the different areas you have to offer.
- Identify those lawyers in the firm with whom you have a built-in reason to cross-sell and/or a personal desire to cross-sell.
- Make a point, at least once a year, to visit other offices in the firm to have meetings with specific partners, attend other practice group meetings and walk the hallways.
- Ask colleagues who have referred their clients to you how their clients have felt about your services – no one will refer you more work if the work they referred was not handled well.
- After careful research, for those clients that you and your colleagues have identified as potential cross-sell targets, devise an action plan to meet with each target client, explore needs and opportunities based on the input that your colleagues have provided and follow up with introductions and requested information.
- Create or join a client team or industry group. These are the two frameworks in firms that naturally facilitate cross-selling and cross-servicing.
- Make it a team endeavour. It is much easier to sell others than to sell yourself, but it is even easier to sell them if they are with you in person. Don't try to do all the selling yourself. Let your colleagues participate in the process of identifying as well as addressing additional client needs.
- Ensure that you really offer value when you cross-sell. Not every client will need what your colleagues have to offer, and there may be many other firms or lawyers that can better serve them in certain areas. Often, it can be difficult to displace another lawyer or firm, even if the client is not fully satisfied. In any event, don't oversell yourself or the firm. However, if the client truly needs something that you or a colleague is superbly qualified to provide, proceed enthusiastically.

One of the things I do judge law firms on is how well they 'play in the sandbox' with other law firms. From a loyalty standpoint, I'm more likely to stick with a firm that I know will let me assemble the best group of people to help me than I am with a firm that may be really well integrated, but will reject working with another firm as if the other firm were a foreign antibody. So the ability to play well in the sandbox I would put as high or higher than having a supposedly synergistic relationship inside a firm.

Mark Chandler
Executive vice president, chief legal officer and chief compliance officer, Cisco Systems, Inc

V. THE ROLE OF COLLABORATION

1. Introduction

Law firms are often described as a collection of sole practitioners practising law under the same roof. This description is fairly accurate in law firms in which partners compete with each other for origination credit and want to maintain control of work and hoard billable hours. Fortunately, many firms now recognise that collaboration and multi-disciplinary teams create better solutions for clients; bring diversity of thought into problem solving; enhance workforce engagement and commitment; and lead to greater profitability and stickier client relationships.

Even if lawyers are more comfortable working alone, we know that clients prefer lawyers who work well with them and with the other law firms that they use, so becoming more collaborative is a critical skill for lawyers to learn.

Developing the mindset and behaviours that support collaboration can be challenging, however. We know the following from Dr Larry Richard:[19]

- Lawyers score very low on sociability when compared to the general public: 12.8% for lawyers versus 50% for the general public. This trait is described as "a desire to interact with people, especially a comfort level in initiating new, intimate connections with others". Low scores on sociability are reflected in lawyers' (dis)inclination towards teamwork and collaboration.
- Lawyers score unusually high on autonomy (89% versus 50% for the general public). According to Richard, "it's common for lawyers to resist being managed, to bridle at being told what to do, and to prize their independence".
- Law firms and lawyers are both highly risk averse and resist new approaches on untested concepts or approaches.
- Lawyers are competitive. They don't do well cooperating with 'the enemy'– that is, other law firms or lawyers.
- Lawyers also score very high on scepticism (90% versus 50% for the general public). According to Richard:

  Because lawyers are so skeptical, they tend to shoot down good ideas before they get off the ground. They can also be suspicious of others' motives, thus making it harder to build the level of trust required to sustain collaboration. This is a major impediment to collaboration. But it's not insurmountable – skepticism is an inherently learned trait for the most part, and the most successful lawyers have learned how to use it selectively, and how to dial it back at times when a trusting demeanor is more appropriate.

2. Collaboration is good for clients
Collaboration provides multiple benefits to clients. With the level of complexity of practice specialties and the business problems that clients have, it is rare that one lawyer or even a team in one practice group can holistically address a client's business problems.

There are several opportunities for law firms to collaborate on a client's behalf:

- within the firm, between partners in different practice groups and/or different offices and countries;
- within the firm, between lawyer teams and other professionals with experience in pricing, project management, process and technology;
- between the law firm and its clients' in-house lawyers and business teams;
- between the lawyers and other service providers that serve the client (eg, management and subject-matter consultants, vendors, accountants and bankers); and
- with all other law firms of the client, working together collaboratively as necessary on a matter or deal. DuPont and Pfizer were early adopters of requiring their panel firms to share knowledge and work together, and decades later many in-house counsel have adopted this model.

The most effective way to solve a very complex problem is by having my outside lawyers collaborate deep inside their law firm itself, but also collaborate with both my in-house team and my business team, so that they understand and solve the business problem. With a collaborative team, we definitely get a better result than a group of single specialists each doing their piece.

Chief legal officer, consumer products multinational

The lines between who does what in a matter are blurring, notes one general counsel: "I am looking for my firms to willingly work with me to find the best person or team to efficiently and at the lowest cost address my legal needs. I want my lawyers that work with me to be fluid and flexible in how teams are put together. There are many instances where I want to be involved in matters myself."

Collaboration in problem solving among specialists with different skills, experience and backgrounds brings diversity of thought. Diverse perspectives usually stimulate more creative and innovative solutions to problem solving.

For the past 10 years or so, Harvard scholar Heidi Gardner[20] has conducted extensive research in the area of collaboration in professional service firms. In her book, *Smart Collaboration: How Professionals and Their Firms Succeed by Breaking Down Silos*, she suggests that at the higher end of legal advice and transactions, clients benefit from and appreciate a more collaborative approach to the legal advice and representation they receive.

Gardner summarises 10 reasons why clients value a team approach:

- access to the firm's best knowledge and experts;
- a deeper understanding of their own business;
- insights from across the sector;
- innovation;
- a global perspective;
- collaborative capacity;
- consistency;
- simplicity in the 'vendor base';
- efficiency and economy; and
- relationships and respect.

3. Collaboration leads to higher profits and better served, more loyal clients

Gardner's research also confirms that clients that are served by multiple partners are more loyal and apt to stay with that firm even if the partner leaves: 72% of single partner clients would seek another provider if the relationship partner left the firm, but 90% of multiple partner clients would remain loyal to the existing firm even if the relationship partner left.

"Collaboration brings additional value even to the more routine work, as it helps to drive coordinated project management and efficiency."

But in stark contrast to this very smart business approach, Gardner found that 90.9% of firms still have a single relationship partner engaged with a client. This clearly is an area on which firms should focus their efforts. Gardner's research also substantiates that when more practices are involved in servicing a client, there is exponential growth in revenue to the firm, such that 1+1 = 4. The figures are similar for international firms doing cross-jurisdictional work: client projects involving offices in several countries are significantly more lucrative than single office engagements. Gardner acknowledges that this type of holistic approach is not as practical or affordable for routine legal work, but is very valuable for more complex clients and legal problems, and allows partners to further develop their roles as strategic and trusted advisers. Collaboration brings additional value even to the more routine work, as it helps to drive coordinated project management and efficiency.

4. Cross-selling is not the same as collaboration

We discussed cross-selling in the previous chapter and concluded that cross-serving is a better way to explore additional needs the client may have that require additional or cross-disciplinary knowledge. The type of collaboration discussed by Gardner, however, anticipates that clients are served by multi-disciplinary teams, because often their problems require a range of skillsets and knowledge. Cross-selling, on the other hand, more often involves a partner who is working on one issue being asked for or proposing an introduction to a partner in a different practice area. While this is an easy way to grow a firm's representation of a client, it does not produce the same level of revenue per client as integrated services, according to Gardner.

Finally, Gardner also found that collaboration among large numbers of partners on client matters and relationships also results in much greater revenue origination generated by those partners. Revenue was at least four times greater for individual partners who brought more partners from outside their practice into a client matter than those who brought in fewer partners in total.

VI. COMMITTING TO DIVERSITY TO EARN LOYALTY

1. Introduction

The legal industry – like many others, including financial services, accounting and engineering – has traditionally been a white, male-dominated field. While many firms have focused on and made progress in hiring, retaining and advancing women into leadership roles in firms, the numbers are still strikingly low; even more so when one looks at the number of equity partners and top rainmakers.

The percentage of other diverse attorneys – those of colour or with LGTBQ+ status – is even lower still. And even when firms succeed in recruiting diverse lawyers, they often see higher rates of attrition.

Efforts by companies to force more diversity in law firms began as early as 1992, when DuPont changed its outside law firm and vendor hiring criteria to include diversity as one of the four criteria on which it would base decisions. Tom Sager – associate general counsel at the time and eventually the company's general counsel for many years – continued to implement and improve on efforts to reinforce DuPont's diversity commitment. DuPont's strategic partnership with its panel firms was long admired for many of the innovative approaches it took; and in the area of diversity, it helped its law firms by supporting minority job fairs and incentive programmes, such as its annual diversity awards dinner.

In 1999, the chief legal officers of about 500 major corporations signed a document entitled *Diversity in the Workplace – A Statement of Principle*. This effort was led by the then general counsel of BellSouth Corp, Charles Morgan. In 2004, Roderick Palomar, then general counsel at Sara Lee Corporation, initiated a renewed effort to encourage and hold law firms accountable for their commitment to diversity that resulted in a call to action, which 60 top legal officers signed. At the time, Sager was quoted as saying: "We need to use constructive and creative means to ensure that all of our firms make immediate and lasting advances in the area of diversity in the profession. Failing that, we will need to re-examine those relationships where progress has not been achieved with a view of placing work elsewhere." He also noted that if firms did not comply, there would be repercussions.[21] Palomar was among the first legal department leaders to 'fire' an outside law firm for its lack of progress and commitment towards diversity.

In 2016, the American Bar Association enacted Resolution 113 to help promote diversity in the legal profession[22] and to help clients hold their law firms accountable. In 2019, 170 general counsel and chief legal officers signed a letter addressed to the law firm community reiterating their commitment to D&I, and confirming

At the end of the day, we want our service providers to represent the communities we serve. This value commitment comes from the top with our CEO and we all live these values. We have spent time figuring out what issues make it difficult to engage lawyers from diverse backgrounds and how we can improve. We expect law firms to succeed in improving the diversity of their lawyers. We now have data from our e-billing system from our outside firms on the lawyers from underrepresented backgrounds working on our matters and where they are located. Our organisation's supplier diversity initiative has a stated goal of reaching a percentage of black and other lawyers from underrepresented backgrounds working on our matters and in the communities we serve. We have also started working with firms to support and provide opportunities to lawyers from underrepresented backgrounds to help them advance.

David Mack
Senior vice president and chief legal officer, Hartford HealthCare

that they would give more of their legal work to firms that made efforts and progress in these areas. As the letter states: "We, as a group, will direct our substantial outside counsel spend to those law firms that manifest results with respect to diversity and inclusion, in addition to providing the highest degree of quality representation. We sincerely hope that you and your firm will be among those that demonstrate this commitment."[23]

There has been some progress to date; but – as evidenced by the number of such letters and pledges authored and signed – the profession as a whole is still failing to make significant gains in the area of D&I. Many in-house departments now require firms to provide metrics on diversity in RFPs. Clients that do not issue RFPs – most often because they have concluded a preferred panel convergence process – still require a metrics-based report annually and expect to see diversity on the teams they engage on their matters. The challenge is that while some companies have developed incentive and rewards programmes to honour those firms that have done an outstanding job of improving diversity, few clients penalise or fire firms that consistently perform poorly on diversity.

General counsel acknowledge that they cannot make wholesale change right away. Black general counsel in particular say that they often feel pressure to hire black outside lawyers, but cannot do so just because they share ethnicity. The lawyer must still have the competence and expertise that general counsel need, and must provide the same or greater service as the incumbent lawyers they use, in order to consider a change. An additional hurdle is that many companies that hire law firms have not achieved diverse representation in their own senior executive ranks or in-house legal departments, which makes it more difficult to demand this of their outside firms.

2. Diversity as a component of client loyalty

Clients are again trying to assert themselves with law firms to demand greater effort and transparency around the hiring, retention and assignment of diverse lawyers to their matters. In 2020, after the George Floyd protests, 127 law firms formed the Law Firm Antiracism Alliance. Too often, however, these efforts enable in-house departments and law firms to 'check the box' and pay lip service to improving diversity and equity without being held accountable. But some companies really are trying to change the status quo by demanding more diversity and equity.

Several legal departments have initiated formal methods of evaluating and rewarding their law firms for progress (or lack thereof) on the diversity front.

We are leading the way in pushing the legal community to publicly share D&I data and we're driving a totally new D&I metric to measure the firms with which we do business. Leaders in our legal department – including General Counsel Ivan Fong and Assistant General Counsel Eric Rucker, the chair of our D&I committee – concluded that tracking hours of diverse lawyers was ineffective. Instead, they proposed that each of our preferred counsel network firms appoint either a relationship partner or a successor who is diverse. We now require this from all of our preferred counsel network firms. This purposeful succession planning ensures that diverse lawyers have real influence within their firms, and that we have diverse perspectives represented in our work. It is simple, easy to track and it works.

Maureen Harms
Associate general counsel and managing counsel, 3M Co

The following companies have mandated diversity as an important criterion of loyalty:

- Intel's IntelRule is described on its website as follows: "Beginning Jan. 1, 2021, Intel will not retain or use outside law firms in the US that are average or below average on diversity. Firms are eligible to do legal work for Intel only if, as of that date and thereafter, they meet two diversity criteria: at least 21% of the firm's US equity partners are women and at least 10% of the firm's US equity partners are underrepresented minorities (which, for this purpose, we define as equity partners whose race is other than full white/Caucasian, and partners who have self-identified as LBGTQ+, disabled or as veterans)."[24]
- Microsoft has designed a programme to support and reward its strategic partner law firms using key metrics that measure diversity at the firm, diversity in leadership positions and diversity on its legal matters. It now awards a 2% bonus to firms that meet specific diversity metrics.[25]
- Facebook instituted a requirement in 2017 that its outside legal teams be comprised of at least 33% women and ethnic minorities, and demonstrate specific and measurable opportunities for leadership.[26]
- Hewlett-Packard has initiated a 10% hold-back of fees if its firms do not have at least one diverse relationship partner or attorney billing comprising at least 10% of the billing on its matters.[27]
- MetLife requires its firms to provide sponsorship for its diverse talent; firms are measured annually for improvements and, if placed on an 'accountability' alert, must work with the general counsel on an improvement plan or risk losing a place on its preferred provider panel.[28]
- AT&T also holds back a portion of a firm's fees, which is paid out only after data in an annual survey confirms that the firm has improved in its metrics.[29]
- Xcel Energy has developed a preferred panel firm peer-ranking matrix. While the firms are not identified, each panel firm can see how it compares to its peers relative to diversity criteria.[30]
- Engage Excellence is a programme co-founded by DuPont, General Mills, Verizon and Walmart, in which the legal departments commit a percentage of their outside legal spend to firms that demonstrate diverse teams that serve as lead counsel on their matters.[31]

Law firms also are working hard to make improvements. Diversity Lab[32] is an organisation founded by Caren Ulrich Stacy that designs innovative initiatives to boost inclusion and cultivate diversity in elite law firms and legal departments. Diversity Lab profiles high performers through data techniques that are used to identify, develop, test, measure and re-test new recruitment, advancement and retention initiatives that promote diversity at the leadership level. Through programmes such as Mansfield Rule Certification for law firms, MovetheNeedle, the OnRamp Fellowship and Women in Leadership Hackathons, Diversity Lab has helped law firms and in-house departments to follow more stringent and specific guidelines for improved D&I results.

A number of other in-house departments are strengthening their resolve to hold law firms accountable for progress in building and supporting diverse legal teams. This commitment and the resulting requirements of law firms that serve these companies will likely serve as the starting point for law firms that want to earn client loyalty in the future. As noted by one associate general counsel: "We do measure our law firms every year on their diversity metrics. Many of them have diverse teams, but not necessarily at the equity partner level. We partner with our firms on diverse law clerk internships, but we have not actually hired or fired a law firm for not making adequate progress on its diversity initiatives."

As previously discussed, PERSUIT is an RFP software platform that is used by many legal departments. In addition to the benefits it affords legal departments in selecting a panel firm for specific matters, it has enabled companies to further their D&I goals by requiring firms to respond to a series of questions and metrics when completing an RFP.

The types of criteria that PERSUIT helps companies to measure include the following:

- Quantitative D&I metrics:
  - What percentage of lawyers working on the client's matters are diverse (eg, "We require that 30% of all timekeepers on our matters are diverse – women, minority and LGBTQ+")?
  - What percentage of hours (and/or spend) are to be completed by historically underrepresented populations?
  - What percentage of the origination credits go to those diverse lawyers (eg, a diverse partner received 100% of the origination credits)?
  - Are the client's panel firms doing a good job promoting diverse lawyers – what percentage of firm partners are women and what percentage of firm partners are part of a minority?
  - How much is the client spending with diverse-owned law firms (eg, 10% of spend goes to National Association of Minority and Women Owned Law Firms certified diverse law firms)?

Through the Leadership Council for Legal Diversity, we connected with a black, female partner at one of our core firms. She is a non-equity partner hoping to be elevated to equity and the firm is trying to offer her opportunities to expand work from some of its key clients. We set her up to meet with several of our senior lawyers and other executives in the company. In a recent litigation matter, we used PERSUIT for the RFP, and the firm won the matter in part because it committed to give that work to the black, female partner to run. There is no guarantee that this matter will be what advances her to equity partner; but it is tangible that we could help support and advance her, and an example of how we share this value with one of our key law firms.

Melissa Lauderdale-Ward
Chief of staff to Thomas O'Neill, senior vice president and general counsel, Exelon

- Qualitative D&I metrics:
  - Which attorneys working on a client's matters are diverse and what role will they play?
  - Is your firm or company a certified business entity in one or more of the following categories (if yes, please provide certification)? Small business; veteran or disabled veteran-owned business; women-owned business; minority-owned business enterprise, disabled owned business, LGBTQ+-owned business; Women's Business Enterprise National Council; National Minority Supplier Development Council; US Business Leadership Network; National LGBT Chamber of Commerce.

Part 6. Interviews with industry leaders and innovators

I. Jeff Carr, former senior vice president and general counsel of Univar Solutions and FMC Technologies, and inventor of the ACES Model

Jeff Carr frequently quotes US Army General Chief of Staff Eric Shinseki when he says: "If you dislike change, you're going to dislike irrelevance even more." Jeff notes that the delivery of legal services today does not provide the services that customers need in the way they need them – that is, actionable and affordable. He believes that only 15% of what a general counsel needs is bespoke and high value – the type of expertise and advice that a trusted adviser provides. Most of what is needed is competency, scale and affordable headcount; and he believes that companies can do most of this work in-house or find a low-cost provider. "It is incumbent upon lawyers to change what we do, how we do it, how we price it and how we deliver it," he says. "It really comes down to productisation of the vast majority of what we're trying to do."

Jeff goes on to describe the vision and mission of his prior law departments:

> *Our vision is quite simply that every legal problem can be prevented. Our mission is legal optimization: problems prevented and value delivered. This requires taking a group of legal*

professionals and other professionals and forming them into a team to help the company achieve its objectives while maintaining the ethical compass, removing obstacles, leveraging creative disequilibrium and really reinventing what we do and how we do it.

In terms of how to change the current model, Jeff suggests: "We have to change how we train people, how we hire people, how we promote people, how we reward people, how people think and how they work." He believes that the end point has to be customer service – and it's not customer service in the way that lawyers and the legal profession usually define it. It is not excellence in law; it is not interesting legal questions. Instead, it focuses on the following questions:

- What is the problem that the customer needs to solve?
- What is the customer's objective?
- What are the service level expectations?
- What can the customer afford?

If we start by focusing on those elements – on what customers actually need and want, rather than what lawyers think they need and want – we can change how we do things.

There is a fundamental misalignment of interests in the existing billable hour model, argues Jeff:

The only way to reconcile that alignment is to recognise that these billing systems encourage counterproductive behaviour. The compensation and promotion systems in firms that have billable hour targets incentivise lawyers to overwork a file, because that is what they get paid to do. No customer wants to buy hours. They want solutions and results; outputs, not inputs; results, not activity. And yet, problematically, our whole legal delivery system is geared towards providing activity and inputs. It is largely designed to respond to threats and disputes – things that no customer really wants. It is up to customers to force firms to change this business model.

We still don't have a really good way to recognise and reward people who do their jobs well every single day by preventing problems from arising. Unfortunately, people often prefer to be heroes by saving others in trouble. A doctor would rather be a hero and save a life. A lawyer would rather win a lawsuit.

And Jeff goes even further when it comes to the engagement of legal service providers. He wants business-to-business relationships, as opposed to attorney-to-client relationships. He is a contrarian who prefers to hire the firm, not the lawyer. In fact, he virtually never uses the word 'client' – preferring 'customer' instead.

"We have to change how we train people, how we hire people, how we promote people, how we reward people, how people think and how they work."

Jeff Carr

He maintains that most legal services are fungible and most providers are interchangeable in terms of credentials and credibility – the first two elements in his '3Cs' of hiring. That said, he values relationships with those that share the most important of the 3Cs – culture:

> *I look for firms that aren't 'hotels' of siloed lawyers working under the same roof, but have a firm culture that focuses on their service delivery platform. I'm looking for practical, actionable advice from my law firms. Most of the time, I don't need to know how smart you are, because frankly, I'm not interested in interesting questions of law. I've hired you – whether you're inside or outside – because I know you're an expert in the area. So you don't need to convince me about how smart you are; you just need to give me an answer or tell me there isn't an answer and what you would recommend.*

1. The delivered value concept

Everything that Jeff does is encapsulated in one key element of his legal team's mission: delivering value. He sums this up in the equation:

DV=E3

or

Delivered Value = Effectiveness + Efficiency + Experience

Jeff explains how this breaks down as follows:

- 'Effectiveness' means, quite simply, whether the customer's objective is achieved. This requires the customer to be very clear from the outset about the objective of the specific project (what lawyers like to call 'engagements'). The customer must be able to define the problem that is being addressed – whether that be a dispute, an acquisition, a commercial agreement or any number of business or personal challenges with a legal component. Sometimes the customer may not know what a legal problem is, as opposed to some other kind of challenge; great counsellors can help them to figure that out. Trusted advisers know what's within the scope of legal and what's not, and can help to direct the customer to other subject-matter experts as necessary – or simply get out of the way if it's not fundamentally a legal challenge.
- 'Efficiency' is also simple: "What did we agree this was going to cost and what did it actually cost?" Of course, at times the scope may be uncertain and the dreaded cost-plus model may be appropriate; but this is where efficiency in incurring costs is even more important. Activity that's 'nice to have' or that 'might be useful', while remunerative to the firm, is almost never in the interests of the customer.
- 'Experience' is not the lawyer's experience or credentials – what lawyers and law firms love to highlight in their websites and marketing materials; it is rather the experience of the customer with the provider. Granted, this is subjective; but then again, lawyers are in the customer service business. These elements can be defined and agreed: "Return my calls and texts; don't send me new people all the time; respect that time is my most precious commodity." Understand that customers need practical, actionable advice and solutions; if there are options, provide recommendations, not laundry lists. In Jeff's words, be "a one-handed lawyer, as opposed to one who says, 'Well, on the one hand, this; and on the other hand, that.'"

Engagements that are based on these three concepts are those that are both sustainable and valuable.

2. The ACES Model

The ACES Model is precisely this kind of system. On its face, according to Jeff:

> *It's devilishly simple. It forces me and my team, as the customer, to actually define what we want – in terms of both the objective and the service level expectations. And then with that in place, it requires us to give feedback to the service provider about how*

> *they're doing and how they're meeting those requirements as we've defined them.*

Jeff suggests that the model works with any kind of fee engagement – hourly, fixed fee, bands, it makes no difference. He explains: "It simply says, 'You bill us; we're going to pay you 80 cents on the dollar; we're going to hold back 20; and then we're periodically going to give you a report card on three factors: effectiveness, efficiency and experience" – the very same elements of the delivered value concept discussed above.

Jeff continues:

> *These three factors are equally weighted and, based on how you do on your report card, you get between zero and 200% of the amount withheld. Why did we pick 20% as a withholding? That's simple: 20% is enough of a traditional law firm's profit margin for the firm to pay attention. Why did we say zero to 200%? Also simple: it's because we're not looking for a discount; we're actually looking to reward exemplary behaviour. The interesting thing about the report card system is that it's one of the ways I hold my in-house team members accountable for their budgets, because I can't run every matter in the department – and nor should I. I can't meet my expectations to be on budget unless my entire team meets theirs.*

"Trusted advisers know what's within the scope of legal and what's not, and can help to direct the customer to other subject-matter experts as necessary – or simply get out of the way if it's not fundamentally a legal challenge."

Jeff Carr

Something that we realised in implementation is that most evaluation systems are biased and inherently flawed. Our system, like many, uses a five-point scale, from 1 (unacceptable) to 5 (exceptional). Systems like these invariably yield a bimodal distribution – where everybody's either bad (a 1) or great (a 5). That simply is incorrect, because in reality, the majority of service providers are average – a 3. This arises when there are no consequences from doing evaluations.

What I didn't realise when we set up this system is that if one of my lawyers gives somebody above a 3, they are going to pay more than the bill; so if on average they give a 4, they're going to pay 110% of the invoice. If they give somebody a 5, they're going to pay 120% of the invoice.

So for them to meet their budgetary expectations and be on budget, they only have two options: reduce overall spend to fund bonus payments to this and other providers; or take 20% from someone else so that the weighted average score is a 3 and is therefore 100% of projected spend. That immediately forced my lawyers first to do the evaluations and then second to give realistic evaluations. It requires budgetary discipline and eliminates 'grade inflation' – or what some call the 'Lake Woebegone Effect', where everyone is above average.

When we first built the ACES Model, we were not looking for a way to pay less for a better result and better performance; we would actually pay more. If people were outperforming, we would pay 20% more than what they billed us; but in the aggregate, that money would go down. As people provided better service – meaning actually giving us what we need, instead of what they think we need – our overall costs would go down. And that's exactly what happened at FMC Technologies over the course of a decade. Our legal spend declined by 33% in absolute terms, while the company tripled in size; and yet we paid our outside legal providers on average 107% of invoices. The only way to make that math work is by changing what you do, how you do it and how you pay for it. We bought fewer hours, better quality, more effectiveness, more efficiency and a better customer experience. In other words, we created a system that reflects and operationalises the delivered value concept. We created a holistic system that requires communication, feedback, honesty and continuous improvement; we created a context and platform for these incredibly important conversations.

II. Mark Chandler, executive vice president, chief legal officer and chief compliance officer, Cisco Systems, Inc

1. On whether loyalty exists and how it is earned

I don't think my own perception of loyalty has changed over the last 10 years. There are a number of factors that go into building long-term relationships between law firms and law departments and their general counsel. One of the principal elements is trust. Trust plays out in several different ways. First, trust means that you think the work will get done well and you will get the services that you need. Part of that is on you, in being careful what you hire people for. General counsel are getting more selective about the skillset match. In a trusting relationship, you are forgiving if things get screwed up: it didn't work out well, but that's okay, because you know you hired the right person. There is an element of loyalty in that.

2. On cross-selling and the benefits of using the same firm

I personally don't think cross-selling is very effective. When I want to know who to hire for an ancillary matter or a completely different matter and I'm talking to someone who I trust at a large firm, I will often ask, "Who would you recommend if your firm couldn't do the work?" I know they will normally tell me, "My partner down the hall is the best person you could hire to do this." There are economic incentives, social incentives, all kinds of incentives to do so; so you've got to discount it, and I do. There is an expression in the manufacturing world that I live in: "Never believe a vendor, except when they say, 'I can't.'" In fact, when someone says, 'I can't,' you are more likely to believe them the next time they say, 'I can.' So, to your question of loyalty: if I hire a specific firm to do a specific matter, and later they say, "You should really hire my partner to do this other matter," but I don't, this doesn't mean I'm being disloyal. There might have been more of a tendency to do one-stop shopping in the past.

In terms of the possible advantage of using the same firm for multiple different matters, I don't buy that there is 'institutional knowledge' of a company. There may be synergies that are worth considering: is there a level of cooperation required on a particular matter where you believe that people who are at the same firm are better integrated and able to work together than people who are in different firms? Do they have better access to information because of technology, or because they are in the same office and inclined to like each other more?

For example, suppose I hire Firm A in the US to help me with an antitrust action against another company that is misbehaving in the marketplace. I also want to look at the options in Europe. I have a great antitrust partner in Washington from Firm A working for me and I also need someone in Brussels to evaluate this in the European context.

Within the antitrust group at Firm A, I might believe that they have spent time together and know each other and work well. In reality, I don't know if the Brussels lawyer likes or hates her partner in Washington. There are institutional incentives for them to get along together, but I am going to evaluate that on a case-by-case basis. I'm in the computer networking business, and if the antitrust partner in Washington has a lot of experience in hardware and wants me to talk to someone in Brussels who does pharma work, but I know someone at another firm who actually knows all the players in my space, I'm going to want to work with that person. That's what I mean about cross-selling as not being so effective; but I don't see it as disloyal to hire the best folks for the job at hand.

One of the things I do judge law firms on is how well they 'play in the sandbox' with other law firms. From a loyalty standpoint, I'm more likely to stick with a firm that I know will let me assemble the best group of people to help me than I am with a firm that may be really well integrated, but will reject working with another firm as if the other firm were a foreign antibody. So the ability to play well in the sandbox I would put as high or higher than having a supposedly synergistic relationship inside a firm.

"As lawyers, we are very well trained in an educational system through a case method that is based on pathology: the only reason that something is being litigated is because something went wrong."

Mark Chandler

There are some situations in which I might conclude that there are institutional reasons why hiring the same firm would work better – for example, if the people have a long history working together and will have access to a huge amount of data to do the job properly. But that involves an analysis of the synergies on a case-by-case basis, not a question of loyalty *per se*.

3. On the role of partners as trusted advisers

People who have been in a lot of boardrooms will have insight and savvy about how to best utilise the skills of the board, identify issues that will likely come up and help you avoid traps. In general, because of their role, law firms tend to focus on a level of risk aversion that is not helpful when you are making corporate decisions. As lawyers, we are very well trained in an educational system through a case method that is based on pathology: the only reason that something is being litigated is because something went wrong. When I do my presentations to my department, new hires and outside groups, my first slide always says, "The riskiest action is often no action." Worrying about the things that can go wrong is useful to fine tune your approach; but when it dominates, it can create a bias towards inaction.

I once had a situation where I consulted with a partner at a firm about a decision being made by my board of directors. He pointed out a theoretical risk and I presented that to the board, and it ended up concerning people on the board. When we dug into this, it turned out to be a very low risk – it was a purely theoretical concern; so I had to walk this back to have a balanced decision. It wasn't wrong as a thought exercise; but when you looked at the real-world data, there was no sign that it would actually happen. It didn't have anything to do with doing something legal or illegal; it was purely a judgement call.

The ability to work effectively with a board also depends on the person. The principal skill I've developed, having been general counsel for the better part of 32 years – 25 of which for a Fortune 500 public company – is hiring people smarter than I am, so that I have access to critical information and perspectives that I could not come up with myself. The second is that I'm reasonably well able to recognise when something is going to matter or not matter. The most helpful thing I can do when people bring a problem to me is be able to credibly and correctly say, "Don't worry about it. Just do it; it's not going to be an issue."

Sometimes you do get problems that come up and you don't have enough experience on that type of issue. Then it can be helpful to turn to someone in the law firm who has been down that road a few times, and who can look at you and say, "Don't worry about it" or "That could be a problem." That kind of relationship is critical. There are some people who are really, really good at that. They've been in numerous boardrooms, have taken scores of companies public and have really good instincts about what's going to matter and what's not going to matter. Having a really good person like that at your side is really helpful sometimes.

But that doesn't mean that when I have an employment law matter, I'm going to hire the firm with which I have a corporate relationship. They may have people who are really good at employment matters, but sometimes you want a particular skillset or approach to handle that matter, so you go to someone else. I don't believe that is a loyalty issue.

4. On transaction cost and switching risk
There is, of course, a flipside to the loyalty question, which involves transaction cost and switching risk. Sometimes it's a case of better the devil you know! People can be averse to switching firms for fear that it could make things worse. If things are going pretty well and I don't have a strong basis to know for sure that things would be better with another firm, it's sensible to continue working with who I know.

5. On what makes relationships sticky
The 'loyalty' construct doesn't really resonate with me as a motivation to work with a law firm and continue working with a law firm. But some factors that do drive 'stickiness' with my law firms include the following:

- Are they willing to say when they can't do the work?
- Do they have an appreciation of the business context I'm in? Do they understand the business decisions I'm making, so that they aren't just answering a legal question – they are answering a business question? I've described my job as "giving common-sense business advice informed by a knowledge of legal principles". I use law firms to make sure I get the black letter of the law right, if I'm not sure or confused about it. The great law firms will take this one step further and help me answer the business question.
- Am I getting value for money and how do I know? Are they willing to work on a basis that is tied to my success – not that they bear my business risk, but they put their money where their mouths are in terms of outcomes? This is particularly true in the litigation space: how much of your fee are you willing to take on outcome? I've moved almost everything of significance to a fixed fee. Mine is a big enough company in volume that if one deal doesn't work out, the next one will; and as long as they are making money, they're happy. It has to be fair and be a partnership. That really builds loyalty, because then I don't have

"I use law firms to make sure I get the black letter of the law right, if I'm not sure or confused about it. The great law firms will take this one step further and help me answer the business question."

Mark Chandler

> to think about the money. I don't then go out for bids on everything I have, because I know this is a team I like; I know they are competent; and I know I'm getting value for my money and I don't think I'd get a better deal from someone else.

We don't have a formal panel structure, but we have three to four firms on the litigation side; and when other matters come up, we figure out if we need another firm. Sometimes my staff are more risk averse than I am. I always have to push them. I was recently looking at an M&A deal and a staff member came back and said we should hire a certain global firm; and when I asked why, my staff member said, "Because they have a good reputation." I asked, "Who are you going to be working with?" and he had no idea. I told him to go and survey other firms, and call up some peers to see who they're working with.

We still go out on a matter-by-matter basis. I always am open to working with new people.

6. On what he dislikes

We got sued on a matter in California a few months ago. I received an email from a partner I had worked with when he was in a very good DC firm, and who is now in California. He said, "I'd love to catch up for a virtual coffee when you have time, but I wanted to send you the complaint recently filed against Cisco in the Northern District of California. If you don't yet have counsel, I'd be happy to talk to you about how my firm and I could help you defend this case. Several years ago I represented Company X in a similar case and our team obtained summary judgment on all counts."

My response was that we already had the complaint; that we usually get them very quickly; and that, as was recited in the complaint, the firm had sent us a demand letter two months before requesting action. Of course, we already had counsel for this. Further, there'd been national press on the matter. I view the marketing practice of sending a copy of the complaint to the defendant as borderline disqualifying. The idea that the GC of a Fortune 50 company wouldn't know that his company had been sued in a matter that got national press attention is kind of bizarre.

7. On innovation and technology

A commitment to finding ways to do things cheaper and faster is really important. Some firms have invested heavily in e-discovery; some firms have hundreds of attorneys sitting in off-site warehouses looking through documents. Predictive coding is faster, more accurate and cheaper. The firms doing that will have a competitive advantage. My interest is in who will provide the best solutions at the best cost.

A firm that says, "Here are all the technologies we're developing and investing in" is not as interesting to me as a firm that says, "Here are the results we're getting because of the technology we've invested in." There are a lot of tools out there that aren't particularly effective, are not easy to use or are not getting better results.

Technology solutions need to bring together people, process and technology. You can have the technology; but it has to be part of a process that is accessible and you need the people to be convinced to use it. Getting people to change how they do things is very hard. It has to be fast and intuitive, and show an immediate benefit.

Something that you only use every 90 days and that is a little complicated to learn, when you use it again, you will have forgotten and have to relearn it. That won't be effective. I have that problem internally: I have tools that I've built that people won't use because they don't use them frequently enough, so they have to relearn them each time they use them. When the tools are good, getting them deployed may require a dedicated team of people to specialise in using that tool to support transactions.

8. On diversity

We have committed as a company to ensure that there are diverse panels in our hiring and vendor selection. It matters to us to have diversity in the teams that are doing work for us. It also matters what the culture of the law firm is. One law firm has got a lot of good publicity on what they've done on diversity: they are funding scholarships, doing *pro bono* work and so on. I happened to hire a paralegal who had previously worked at that law firm; she wrote me a note saying that she was so glad to be at a company that walked the talk, because she was tired of being at a firm that talked about what they did for lawyers, but that did do nothing to try to drive diversity across their staff or to create an environment that people wanted to work in.

You have to look more broadly at what firms are doing. It's not good enough to have a diverse person on the deal. We ask questions like: "What is your commitment to full-spectrum diversity across your organisation?" It is ingrained in my department to ask those questions of the firms we work with.

"We have committed as a company to ensure that there are diverse panels in our hiring and vendor selection. It matters to us to have diversity in the teams that are doing work for us. It also matters what the culture of the law firm is."

Mark Chandler

III. Vincent Cordo, former central legal operations officer and global sourcing officer, Shell Oil Co; now chief client development and relationship officer, Holland & Knight

1. On how law firms have developed long-term loyalty
Customer loyalty is a critical focus. The approach that firms are using to put together strategic client teams that help push this forward is a priority. Having the right blend of partners, associates and allied professionals on the team usually lends itself to a more successful outcome. Those that are doing a good job at developing clients by building relationships help to avoid account volume erosion and organically build loyalty. They build institutional connections within the law firms and with the client.

2. On what keeps companies coming back to law firms
There are three primary factors to loyalty. The first is the lawyer-to-lawyer relationships at all levels: top management connections are great, but don't forget about the team under the leadership that needs to know you and your firm. They are the ones asking which firms are to be invited to bid on work. Institutionalising relationships is important; rigour on getting to know others in the business is not optional. Contacts get promotions and shift roles, move on to other companies or retire.

The second is quality and economics: it is not about saving a percent; it is results first. If the client received great value in the services delivered and good value for its spend, the firm stands to build on the portfolio.

The third is value services and the supporting cast: support professionals who make up operations – innovations, billing, pricing teams, for example – who work to help things running smoothly. Much work happens behind the scenes and requires asking the tough questions, monitoring the metrics and challenging the status quo, including ensuring that the legal teams diversify which panel firms get invited to bid and then get selected so that legal spend remains with panel firms.

3. On whether the Big 4 or law companies are eroding clients' loyalty to law firms
The Big Four do extremely well and dominate many areas in the world of consulting, which comes with large budgets and teams needed to support efforts. When it comes to legal services, they really don't perceive in-house legal department spend as a big enough opportunity yet to offer the level of value services, discounting, zero transfer cost proposals, secondments or write-offs on rates that law firms do. They just can't or won't offer that yet; but this doesn't mean they aren't

working on ways to creatively add it to their portfolio. That makes them a potential competitor of firms, but a larger competitor of alternative service providers.

They are onboarding allied professionals who can help; but unlike firms that lack support professionals who get it, the Big 4 need more rainmaker partners who can do this, and I'm not aware of any movement of top-tier practices shifting from firms in this space – for example, prominent practice groups shifting their business out of law firms and into the Big 4 umbrella. In the short term, they are more of a competitor to the ALSP prong. It is going to be a challenge for them to be competitive; they are often seen as the more expensive option.

And then there is the issue of how they will handle conflicts. Those that manage a company's audit work will not have a bite at this apple.

Make no mistake, though, I wouldn't sleep on them. They are working hard to break into the market, hiring experts with various legal operations backgrounds. Some of the dilemmas they need to address include the following:

- Can they bring in top-tier legal practice teams from firms?
- How will they handle conflicts?
- Can they be competitive bidding on legal work?

This business is a small fish in a big pond for them – they will have internal competition for clients spending much more money on consulting and the issue of precedence. If they do alternative fee arrangements (AFAs) in legal for those services, or lock-in rates, why won't they do that for their other services? It is a very fine line they will have to manage. It's all doable; but this is the rub, and it's not an easy decision to just jump in on.

4. On the importance of strategic partnerships/panels to the success of corporate legal functions

At Shell, we had a strategic focus on operational excellence and ways of working. Our message to law firms was that a true partnering relationship was essential to our success and that our legal panel needed to continue to partner with Shell to achieve our objectives by being proactive and in the top quartile of the market.

The law firms on our panel continued to analyse their AFA assignment run rate target of 100% for all their matters, services and processes; and helped us improve our operations internally. They did a wonderful job of keeping an eye on the impact of external events in the industry, such as being our watchdog on regulatory matters and other considerations that may also result in a competitive advantage.

"Organisations have an abundance of very smart and capable members of leadership who are lawyers; adding a senior allied professional with experience in operations who can fit the culture and integrate organically in the system will make the firm or team much stronger."

Vincent Cordo

5. On how firms and companies are staffing innovation and legal operations roles

With the increased role of operations, some firms and companies are moving experienced, practising lawyers into these positions or in some cases non-experienced junior professionals. Finding the appropriate blend of resource background is essential. Getting things right in legal operations requires diversity of skills and experience, which usually is not what previously practising lawyers bring to the table – even with a month's crash course on operations or finance, or a passion for programming applications. Leading teams of allied professionals, getting the most out of the investment, is a very large part of what needs to be managed. The teams need a different type of management and support to understand opportunities to grow. Alternatively, repurposing junior-level professionals with limited background managing strategic integration can leave opportunities uncovered without the right mentoring and support. Time has shown that this is not a 'check the box' hire. Organisations have an abundance of very smart and capable members of leadership who are lawyers; adding a senior allied professional with experience in operations who can fit the culture and integrate organically in the system will make the firm or team much stronger.

I also see a trend where some see innovation or legal operations roles as an opportunity for a career shift – sometimes a temporary move from legal practice that may help to advance into a leadership role as an associate general counsel or senior general counsel. This presents challenges and, in some cases, puts a major a strain on individuals who want to get back into practising law, and makes it hard for full immersion in the role. The other dilemma is to be knowledgeable of those who are not comfortable pushing the barriers needed for change.

Many lawyers, although well-intentioned, are not as effective at managing teams of support professionals as they are at managing their own practice or teams of lawyers. For example, weighting the value of an analytics expert that would be levelled similarly to a senior-level attorney is not something in their wheelhouse. Prioritising countless 'fire drills' is critical in this line of support and may seem mundane to most. Being readily available to staff who need guidance with their career growth can even smother some and, if not managed properly, can hinder the ability to truly capture the team's full breadth of capabilities for the department. This is what makes this type of role so important. Client management requires a team of lawyers who are familiar with a suite of strategy, pricing, data analytics, project management and account planning rigour. Those with traditional backgrounds don't always have the same level of interest in or experience with the many tiers of tasks that come with these delivery models; and operating in an agile way isn't natural for everyone. Also, lawyers are trained to identify risk and resist change; whereas innovation and process improvement require new ideas, agility and speed.

6. On how to use data analytics and metrics to evaluate law firm effectiveness

Data analytics can be very useful tools when firms and in-house teams leverage them proactively as part of their delivery and after-action review model. Clients expect firms – even when this is not the first thing on the list of discussion topics – to use data analytics and key performance metrics to help them stay efficient on tasks. Efficiency is quality and delivery first. It goes beyond the price: the primary focus is cycle time to close out the task. Ultimately, the customer is the driver, and they want to know that all facets of the business are running efficiently. That is important to both the firm and the in-house team. Transparency on the outcomes that the metrics are intended to measure or monitor is what is important on both sides – if there is a change of scope that alters the effort needed on a matter, both sides need the facts to align on a way forward early, not after the matter has concluded. Consistency on both the client side and the firm side is needed for data to be useful – and the entire relationship and portfolio are critical. Firms and in-house departments are now leaning on leveraging allied professionals – such as legal operations, pricing and analytics, function support, project managers, paralegals and admins – to play a role.

At Shell, we measured performance indicators such as whether a law firm delivered on time and on budget over a set timeframe; where the pricing came in; what the end result of the matter was; and other factors – all of which were put into a performance metric that was used when evaluating the legal provider's performance.

If a matter (eg, litigation or a corporate matter) goes beyond expectations, assumptions and estimates, law firms should communicate the change immediately to the in-house lead lawyer and work with their pricing person in advance to communicate why the matter is veering off the proposed budget and how the new scope has increased the timekeeper effort required. It is imperative, as part of the process, to look at the previous time entry up to the point where the scope changed, to see if there were any inefficiencies that impacted the budget. That is much easier for a company to deal with and less trouble for the law firm than working extra time beyond the budget, billing after the fact and then having uncomfortable billing or write-off discussions months later. This all goes to performance scorecard measurement.

Processes and assignments are not taken lightly. At Shell, we audited these metrics and reported on how our panel firms embraced processes that enhanced the efficiency we were looking for – whether through budget performance, outcomes, utilisation of technology or improved workflow processes. The reporting requirements of external counsel continue to advance, so firms are expected to report on results to internal counsel with assurances of high-quality work product at a lower cost and on schedule. Scoring and reporting on overall account management is also a very important component of the relationship.

7. On whether a firm's investment in automation/innovative service delivery impacts on client longevity and loyalty
Yes, absolutely. Automation is always explored. However, even with automation, continued knowledge management on cases is important, so there will always be levels of people time needed to overview the matter. Another important tool we used often was PERSUIT, which streamlined the RFP process between our panel firms and us. It utilises a templated process which helps track budgets, staffing and other key metrics, including D&I.

8. On whether firms that innovate will lose loyalty
When it comes down to it, it's legal competence and outcomes first;

"The argument that lawyers don't want to be efficient due to losing billable hours to innovation is shifting. The truth is that if they aren't using innovation, it is very likely that most of the hours are or will be written off."

Vincent Cordo

innovation comes after. The argument that lawyers don't want to be efficient due to losing billable hours to innovation is shifting. The truth is that if they aren't using innovation, it is very likely that most of the hours are or will be written off. The debate has shifted, leveraging tech to avoid erosion due to write-offs and visually showing clients that the firm is effective at managing key performance indicators – for example, focused on D&I-staffed matters or turning matters around with quality results in top-quartile efficient cycle times. I have never seen a primary push where an in-house team asked me to find an alternative firm with better tech for an opportunity, whether it be a bet-the-company case or even something that could be commoditised. It always comes down to the top-tier lawyer first who can lead the opportunity. Innovation is a very important tool in a great lawyer's toolkit – being more efficient, offering transparency and so on. However, it does not make them great lawyers. Top-tier legal talent is great regardless.

IV. Christopher Marston, founder and CEO, Exemplar Companies

Exemplar Companies was founded by CEO Christopher Marston in 2005 as an alternative to traditional law and accounting firms. With a customer-centric approach, focused on building long-term, loyal relationships, it is a new-economy knowledge firm combining law, tax, accounting and investment banking that advises businesses across the United States. It focuses on accelerating revolutionary game-changers and impact businesses that align with financial, environmental, social and spiritual values. According to Christopher Marston, "We need happy people doing good in the world who spend their life's energy advancing revolutionaries." This added focus on aligning with spiritual values is a unique quality at Exemplar.

Exemplar Companies comprises four service units:

- Exemplar Capital, a licensed broker-dealer;
- Exemplar Law, one of the first in the country to abandon hourly billing in favour of exclusive value-based pricing;
- Exemplar Strategy; and
- Exemplar Tax and Accounting.

As Marston explains, "When I founded the firm, it was so obvious that billing by the hour was so massively misaligned with clients' best interests. I couldn't reconcile this." His response was to launch a new model knowledge firm.

According to Marston, clients benefit from Exemplar's unique value model in two key ways:

> *First, we have the economic power to care and that changes outcomes. We have time to cultivate relationships and get to know our clients. We aren't up against the clock all the time. We go deep with clients and build relationships. Professionals who bill by the hour have to meet quotas – they don't have time to care. They are slaves to the model; they are cogs in the wheel, only as good as the next hour billed. When you use the value model, you can participate in the value you create. It's not a zero-sum game, as it is in the hourly model.*
>
> *Second, being able to approach clients' needs holistically is transformative, as it mirrors the issues that most founders and CEOs face. Everything that goes on in a business's growth is connected, and having knowledge advisers who can help clients across the spectrum of needs changes the outcome. It also transforms the previous negative experiences that many businesses have had from consuming professional services in order to grow a business.*

Marston goes on to outline some of Exemplar's individual service offerings, to illustrate how this distinctive model translates into practice. For example, its Flexpertise® programme adopts a holistic approach to advice, in which the relationship layer is the most important component:

> *It provides the client with access to experts from all service areas, who work together to achieve the client's growth initiatives. At the outset, the client's pressing legal needs, capital options and potential growth pathways are all considered, together with business focus, product focus, legacy/end-game goals, business structure, tax plan and more. The team plans the budget for the next calendar quarter and year to determine the necessary pieces of the puzzle, from inside professional support to outside expertise, including priority and timing of these items. The success of this programme results from ongoing, proactive and client-centric attention and communication.*
>
> *Business Emergency Room® is a new service that helps companies navigate business problems and disruption in real time, in order to support small businesses and emerging enterprises. Businesses around the country have access to a fully staffed triage team*

"We need happy people doing good in the world who spend their life's energy advancing revolutionaries."

Christopher Marston

> *during business hours, with 24-hour turnaround to getting the right professional team members engaged to solve the problem. We are taking leadership to support emerging enterprises and small business in anticipation of the upcoming challenges businesses will face due to economic disruptions during 2020 and beyond.*

And this client-centric approach is also reflected in Exemplar's own systems and processes:

> *Unlike at most law and accounting firms, when a new client is engaged by the firm, it is assigned to someone other than the originating partner/director or the partner performing most of the work. This shifts the focus from self-interest to serving the client. The firm has a professional account manager who meets one to one with the firm's top clients (those in the top 20%) to gauge satisfaction and collect feedback that is acted upon. We also conduct random digital surveys of all clients, to identify any issues with service or quality, and are implementing an automated Net Promoter scoring and professional review.*

Exemplar's core principles reflect the shared values and vision of Marston and his team. One of his key goals is to enable his colleagues at Exemplar to live their purpose. For example, each professional's bio begins with what that person loves about Exemplar. These common values essentially serve as the firm's cultural glue.

And this also extends to embracing the values of clients, as Marston explains: "We show respect to clients' values – social, environmental, spiritual and financial. We focus on achieving success and creating a lasting and trusting relationship with them. We do this because, although we help businesses, at the heart of it all we impact people."

Part 7. Conclusion

I. HEALTHY CLIENT ROADMAP: 25 TIPS TO KEEP CLIENTS HAPPY, SATISFIED AND LOYAL

Despite all the talk about fading client loyalty and clients increasingly pushing matters to the least expensive 'bidder', many things about relationships still matter to most clients. Below is a detailed checklist to help you ensure that your client relationships are and stay healthy.

1. Be pragmatic and commercial
Remember that, as much as your clients may like you and respect you, you represent a cost item in their organisation's budget. Gone are the days when most clients would justify hiring a brilliant expert at all costs. Today, clients evaluate their needs relative to the cost and determine the most effective and efficient way to achieve results. Lawyers who can understand and communicate with clients about their pressures, their business objectives relative to legal strategy and their own internal clients (usually the executives and board) will be much more valued and valuable.

Really understand the client's business and how it operates. Spend a day or two with the client, at their place of business (on your own time/dime). Ask to follow others around, sit in on meetings and meet others on the business side. This investment of time will be appreciated by clients and will provide you and your team with a much better sense of what the business is about and how the legal team interacts with the business.

2. Be empathetic and an avid listener
Focus on clients' needs, interests, agenda, objectives and questions. Put yourself in their shoes to understand what challenges they face inside the job. Be genuine in your interest and listen without interrupting. Don't try to convince clients of all you know or your point of view.

3. Define value and success for each client
Ask each client what criteria they use to determine the value of legal services in general, and then specifically the level of value that you deliver to them and how or why. Be clear on how they will measure your success: what a successful engagement or relationship will look like to them.

4. Get to know your clients and the culture of their organisation
Take time to get to know your clients professionally and personally – their hobbies, passions and life goals. Do some searching online to see what you can find on LinkedIn, Facebook or their company website. Ask for an organisational chart to see how the legal department is

"Ask each client what criteria they use to determine the value of legal services in general, and then specifically the level of value that you deliver to them and how or why. Be clear on how they will measure your success: what a successful engagement or relationship will look like to them."

structured as its own department, but also where it fits in the broader structure of the organisation. Try to get a sense of where your client contact fits within the organisation.

5. Develop client-specific service plans and protocols
When beginning to work with new clients, discuss their preferences for how, with whom and how often to communicate; how they prefer their billing; whether they want to be included in strategy discussions; whether they want status reports and if so, how often and in what format (by email, phone or formal reports).

6. Collaborate to provide the best solution
Clients' problems or matters often require different skills, levels of expertise and price points. There are many options for clients today other than the traditional law firm. In addition to internal collaboration within your own practice groups and among others, proactively consider collaborating with other lawyers, experts and providers to put together the best team and solution. If you don't, clients most certainly will themselves.

7. Use technology, automation and tools that lead to efficiency
Continuously evaluate how effectively you manage client projects by using technology, project management protocols and early case assessment. Stay on top of new trends and products, with an eye towards AI resources and providers that you can partner with.

8. Make use of knowledge management
Most clients assume that by now, firms have created repositories of experience and knowledge so that they don't have to reinvent the wheel each time. Do some research internally and externally to identify prior projects and precedents similar to those which you are handling for clients, including reaching out to colleagues who may have been involved in similar cases or projects. Clients often hire you because you have handled a multitude of cases like theirs in their industry. Demonstrate to clients that you are using that knowledge for direct benefit to them.

9. Scope and budget matters carefully
Break down matters in stages and components, and evaluate prior matters for a delineation of the time and level of skill needed. Prepare budgets for clients that are detailed and that have certain milestones by which you and the client can evaluate progress and status against the budget. All budgets and work in progress should be monitored in real time through automation and should be accessible to clients.

10. Manage expectations
As soon as you begin scoping a project and defining deliverables,

discuss and agree on realistic deadlines and outcomes with the client. Once you begin working on a new matter, keep the client apprised of the status of the project; discuss any roadblocks or expanded scope of work requested or required, especially if it affects the budget; and let the client know when you have added any new professionals to help staff the matter and why.

11. Ensure that your bills are clear, accurate, frequent and transparent

Some lawyers think that billing is an accounting function and that getting bills paid is a collections activity. This couldn't be further from the truth. Clients pay bills when they believe that the value you are delivering is in line with what you both agreed. They hate surprises, such as budget overruns or additional people billing to the file who they have never met. Even worse are bills with errors in them or when time billed is over a month old. Call clients in advance if a bill is likely to be more than you estimated or than they are expecting. Billing is a chance to see how you are doing relative to the client's perception of value and to nurture the relationship.

12. Consider creative value pricing

Don't wait for clients to raise this. Ask them if they are using alternative pricing arrangements now and which ones are working for them and why. If the client is willing, proactively explore retainers, flat or project fees, pricing by stage of work or in buckets of work, and holdbacks with a potential bonus. Remember that most clients prefer predictability so that they can budget for legal expenses in advance, and they most certainly appreciate firms that are willing to put skin in the game and share in some risk.

13. Consider all staffing options

There may be a number of ways in which you could get a project completed on a client's behalf. Be sure to delegate what can be done by lower-cost personnel – lawyers, paralegals, other technical experts or project managers – and by hiring contract staff.

14. Get to know people who are important to the client

Become familiar with other key members of the client's organisation, including assistants. Get to know their immediate circles of influence and importance. Add all relevant contacts to your contact database and categorise them by affiliation to specific clients.

15. Stay in touch regularly and visit your clients

Be in contact with every active client at least once a quarter and preferably every month – especially when you are not working with them on an active matter. You should also plan an in-person visit to your five most active clients at least annually. Walk their hallways, meet some of their colleagues and offer to do a CLE briefing for the team. You will almost always walk away with new business, in addition to earning the appreciation of your client.

16. Be available and accessible

Try to answer your own phone personally. At a time when, technically, you could be available 24/7, determine with the client what is reasonable. Provide your cell phone number, but establish boundaries for when clients should or should not use it. Whatever you do, don't ask your assistant to place a call to a client for you, then have them hold for you. This makes clients feel that your time is much more important than theirs. Set an out-of-office response when you will be away from the office for a day or more. Your message should indicate when you plan to return to the office and who clients should contact in your place.

17. Be responsive

Respond to all emails within four hours of receiving them. If you are not available, ask your assistant to respond for you and indicate when you will respond personally. Make sure that your voicemail is client-friendly and helpful. Voice messages should be updated regularly to let clients know where and how to reach you, or who else they can call.

"Whatever you do, don't ask your assistant to place a call to a client for you, then have them hold for you. This makes clients feel that your time is much more important than theirs."

This shows clients and other callers that you check your voicemail often and that their calls are important. Use a tool that converts phone messages into emails so that you get them in your inbox instantaneously.

18. Ensure that you and your team produce excellent work and service

Keep others informed of the status of matters by sending emails, reminders and copies of correspondence. Avoid last-minute demands of clients. Don't wait to send the client a draft of a document that they see for the first time only 24 hours before it needs to be filed. Share calendars and remind team members in advance of commitments and deadlines. Use project management tools or maintain a tickler system of all ongoing projects and matters for the client, and respective timelines, benchmarks and deadlines. Ensure that all work that goes out is proofread and checked again for typos, grammar and citation accuracy.

19. Give away some free time

Provide some free counselling time and note it on the bill as "General Advice, No Charge". If you manage a team and multiple matters for clients, you will likely also rack up quite a few management hours that cannot be billed. Indicate the amount of time that you and others spend on your invoices and again in an annual summary, so that the client can attach value to this.

20. Seek feedback and input regularly and formally

Regularly ask your clients for feedback on how you and your team could improve your services for them. Ask them whether there are areas in which they are dissatisfied or where the firm could improve. Conduct annual client satisfaction surveys (by email, by telephone or in person) with all clients to get feedback on service. At the completion of each matter, send an end-of-matter questionnaire.

For your largest clients, conduct an annual review, as both a look-back review and a look forward to anticipated needs and priorities.

21. Stay ahead of the curve on trends

Find out and stay informed about the industry, competitive, legislative and regulatory issues that clients are facing. Look for the next big need or trend in your practice niche, market or clients' industries. Read daily news feeds on local and regional issues, as well as business and industry issues that may affect clients. Set up a Google alert or use other tools to send you news daily on key issues, clients, practice trends or industries. Let clients know that you are keeping your finger on the pulse to bring them new ideas or updates about how other clients may be tackling similar problems.

22. 'Look around the corner'
As you track trends, think about client problems proactively. Conduct 'preventative' audits to help identify potential regulatory compliance violations, risks and issues before they become legal problems. Develop a prevention checklist for your clients. Point them to free online resources and information. Pick up the phone and call them about an issue that you have observed with other clients or that you believe is coming down the line.

23. Add value beyond your representation
Offer to do a tailored, free briefing or seminar for in-house lawyers, senior management or the board. Take clients to your business/industry seminars and to important political, civic or business events. Inform your client about a good business deal. Try to put clients together who could share business information and opportunities. Offer to 'lend' or 'second' lawyers and support staff to clients during crunch times – for a week, a month or even a year.

24. Understand your role and value in the client's eyes
Some lawyers serve clients as deep technical experts in a particular area; others more as trusted advisers who share and provide insights on broader business and legal issues. Assess where you fit relative to other law firms and service providers that the client uses, and also what they do themselves internally. One good barometer is to find out what percentage of their outside legal spend your firm receives. The chances are that if it is less than 10% (and many firms are only getting 1% or less), you have less leverage and value, and are likely not considered one of your client's 'partner' firms.

25. Constantly look for ways to help clients
Keep your clients on your radar at all times – whether their legal needs or, just as importantly, their personal agendas and objectives. Help them as they navigate internal politics; try to find a new job; advance their own career and expertise. They may benefit from school and medical referrals, or welcome an introduction to a civic or charitable leadership opportunity. Clients are people who struggle with many of the same challenges that you do. If you are helpful, reliable and resourceful, and produce the results they seek, you will engender loyalty and develop client fans who can become your best salesforce.

Part 8. Appendices

Appendix I. Covenant with counsel[33]

The following are factors that might be considered in structuring relationships. Feel free to add, modify or delete as you wish; or simply use them as a starting point for your own thinking.

As a client, we will:

- Define our objectives in the engagement and advise you if they change.
- Pay your bills promptly.
- Use value-based terms to reward success and efficiency.
- Understand that budgets may need to be revised for unforeseen events.
- Understand that our relationship is built on mutual trust; unless we tell you otherwise, we don't need or want a 'no stone unturned' approach.
- Evaluate your performance fairly and regularly.
- Conduct 'after-action' reviews at the end of each matter to help continuously improve performance.
- Designate one lawyer to serve as our relationship manager.
- Be flexible and accommodating in dealing with potential conflict of interest issues that may arise.

- Provide training opportunities for your associates by discussing creative arrangements upfront.
- Help your firm to better collaborate with other lawyers and law firms.
- Recommend your firm to other companies and potential clients.
- Seek arrangements with our other service suppliers to lower our costs.
- Help to nurture an enduring relationship with the firm, not just individual lawyers.
- Support our own as well as your pro bono and diversity activities.
- Ensure that our legal team 'walks the talk'.

As outside counsel, our firm will:

- Learn your business and strategic objectives and apply that understanding to your matters.
- Give honest feedback on whether your objectives in a matter are realistic and attainable.
- Use the most appropriate staffing and tell you if we don't have the necessary expertise.
- Designate one lawyer to serve as our relationship manager, whose time will not be billed for this role.
- Proactively offer value-based alternative fee structures.
- Provide budgets and estimates for specific engagements upfront and advise you immediately if there may be any material changes.
- Understand that we are responsible for our budgets and estimates, and that our experience forms a basis for accuracy.
- Seek to reduce our costs creatively and constantly, and share those savings with you.
- Understand that you do not seek elegance, new law or perfection, unless these provide value consistent with your company's objectives.
- Train our associates efficiently and effectively without imposing additional and unwarranted costs on you.
- Never 'reinvent the wheel' – we will look first to past work product and encourage efficiency and continuous improvement.
- Not ask for blanket conflict waivers and discuss with you any client or issue conflicts.
- Use technology to our mutual benefit, including billing.
- Meet deadlines and keep in touch.
- Continue our commitment to pro bono and diversity activities.
- Work hard to retain and reward personnel that embrace these concepts, and ensure that every member working on your project 'walks the talk'.

FOR COMPANY BY: FOR LAW FIRM BY:

Appendix II. Guidelines and procedures for outside counsel[34]

1. Procedures for all matters

- We will only work with legal service providers that have been approved and accepted into our Alliance Counsel programme. Adding any new provider to our programme will require the approval of the general counsel.
- All work by our Alliance providers will be done under the Alliance Covenant – we will no longer execute firm engagement letters. In particular, while we will be understanding and liberal in waiving conflicts, we will not provide advance blanket waivers of conflicts. The covenant will serve as the 'frame agreement' between our companies and will be posted to the firm's profile in Legal Tracker (our matter management platform). There will be one, and only one, B2B agreement between and each provider accepted into our Alliance programme.
- Legal Tracker will be the platform used as our primary tool for communication and functional management, including matter management, document management, relationship management and financial management.
- Engagement on specific matters will be through the grant of matter access through Legal Tracker. Notice of matter access will serve as the 'work order' for the project. You should not commence work until you have been granted access to a matter for the project.
- Only a member of the legal team may engage a firm to provide legal services; that said, the specific project manager may not be a member of the legal team and will be designated in the matter profile.
- Before commencing any non-exigent, material work, the objective, scope and budget for the project must be agreed and recorded in Legal Tracker.
- Every matter will be handled by a project team of one or more individuals with specific roles, responsibilities and RACI communication protocols clearly established.
- Budgets will be for the entire life of the matter and the current year. Budgets will be 'all-in', including all expenses or subcontractors.
- All work will be done under the ACES fee model – holdback of 20% of all fees, payment of holdback at 0-200% based on the ACES evaluation (aka the report card), which assesses value delivered on the basis of V= E3 (Effectiveness + Efficiency + Experience). Any matter proposed to be done on any other basis must be approved at inception by the general counsel.
- We focus on project budgets and we expect work to be done by the lowest-cost resources capable of delivering value to us as the customer. This is the essence of E3. Please note that hourly

rates are largely irrelevant to us – but we recognise their utility to firms as a component of costs. That said, while we prefer fixed fee arrangements, we will consider hourly engagements, phased engagements or banded arrangements, so long as they are connected to full matter and current year budgets, and subject to the ACES holdback/assessment/payout.

- On a monthly basis, short matter status reports must be input into the matter status reporting function within Legal Tracker. Invoices cannot be submitted unless status reporting is current. Particularly notable developments – those deserving of being brought to the attention of the general counsel and senior executives of the company – are to be flagged as 'material' in Legal Tracker.
- Invoices will be received and approved for payment electronically through the Legal Tracker platform and must be submitted within 30 days of performance of the work. We will commit to approve invoices timely, but late invoices will be rejected and not paid.
- At the conclusion of a matter, a 'lesson learned' review and evaluation will be conducted by the project manager. We will be looking for procedural improvements in how the team managed the project, as well as substantive improvements designed to change company behaviour and prevent similar problems in the future.
- The Alliance provider's relationship manager will conduct an annual relationship review to cover performance across all matters.

2. Litigation-specific procedures

- Upon initiation, a default budget of [X] shall be established. The supervising attorney may raise or lower this default budget if the circumstances warrant.
- If the matter is not resolved within 90 days, a full case budget, current year budget and exposure analysis are required. Decision tree analysis is the preferred method to develop and present the exposure analysis.
- Case budgets must include all expenses, including experts or other service providers.
- Litigation engagements may be done under either the ACES report card model or the ACES phased budget model.
- Groups of similar cases (eg, mass tort and HR) may be aggregated in a collective annual budget. In other words, each case would have a full matter budget and a $0 current budget; a general matter would have the aggregate current year budget. These individual case costs would be aggregated against the general group budget to gauge budget to actual performance.
- Where appropriate, a range of mock jury resources will be used to validate the risk exposure analysis.

- Settlement authority will be based on delegation of signature authority, with concurrent approval of the supervising attorney or general counsel, as appropriate.

3. IP-specific procedures

- Patent or trademark families will be budgeted for under a single general matter for that family or mark.
- The project manager may agree with the Alliance firm to create individual country-specific matters by country to collect data and expenses for the specific country process. These costs will be aggregated against the general family or mark budget to gauge budget to actual performance.

Appendix III. Steps to conducting effective client interviews[35]

1. Design a good interview guide

In order to solicit meaningful and accurate information, the survey must be carefully crafted. An effective interview will incorporate many characteristics, including the following:

- It includes simple and concise questions, unbiased questions, single issue questions, open and closed-ended questions, and opportunities for clients to explain or elaborate on their answers.
- It requires only 20 to 30 minutes to complete (though many clients seek additional time, so ask the client for their preference).
- It allows for anonymity of response.
- It includes a section that asks the client to rate the firm on a set of 10 to 15 service attributes on a scale of 0-10.
- It has a good sequencing of questions, from broad or general areas (eg, building trust, interest and rapport) to more specific questions that explore more sensitive or difficult areas.

At no time should a feedback interview be hijacked to sell additional services.

It is always a good idea to pre-test your interview guide with three to four clients and then modify it accordingly.

2. Decide which client contacts will be interviewed

Within the client organisation, there may be several individuals with whom various people in the law firm come into contact. While not everyone in the organisation should be asked for input, any and all who have significant interaction and experience with the firm and are senior enough to supervise the intake and outflow of work should be included.

It is wise to ask the primary client contact who else they would like the firm to interview in addition to themselves. Some clients prefer to have one voice and to control the feedback, with the key contact seeking input from others before reporting to the firm. In other instances, they recognise that others have individual perspectives that could be helpful in providing the firm with constructive feedback. The challenge arises if the primary contact does not have as much hands-on experience with the firm and therefore has less specific feedback, but for some reason does not want the firm speaking with others. This will seriously hamper your ability to collect useful and specific feedback.

3. Determine who will conduct the interviews for the firm
There are drawbacks to using the partner who has primary responsibility for or contact with the client, since the goal is to elicit candid feedback about performance, personnel, chemistry and problem areas. Similarly, there may be some clients who feel uncomfortable speaking with a stranger – particularly if the relationship with the primary contact partner is longstanding and very personal.

Often, firms will designate the managing partner, practice group leaders and/or other senior practitioners (sometimes a recently retired partner) to conduct these interviews. Frequently, the chief client officer, chief business development officer (CBDO) or chief marketing officer (CMO) accompanies a partner to the interview, and in many cases may conduct these alone. If your CBDO or CMO does initiate or accompany a partner on the interview, be prepared to give a short explanation to the client for that individual's involvement, with a focus on meeting client needs. Otherwise, clients often assume that the CBDO or CMO is there to sell them more business. The partners who conduct these interviews should be provided with scripts and given training on how to surface and respond to issues, how and when to probe, and how to put clients at ease.

Many firms prefer to use third-party consultants for client interviews. Often, effective consultants can elicit more candid views on sensitive topics of satisfaction, effectiveness, what other firms are doing better and criticisms or concerns.

4. Pre-interview prep: information gathering
The partner who is the primary contact for the client or the client account manager should be responsible for collecting all pertinent information about the client and developing a portfolio of materials. This will include:

- service history, including all lawyers and staff;
- financial history, including revenue, payment patterns and write-offs; revenue should be broken down by practice group and matter, office and income trends (up or down) identified;
- client materials, including annual reports, public company documents filed with regulatory agencies and annual returns, litigation and deal reports, press releases and publicity, company marketing materials, newsletters and so on;
- past service interview and audit summaries; and
- a CRM report on recent client interactions.

5. Pre-interview prep: client team call to review information, potential concerns, opportunities
The client relationship partner should convene a meeting of the team

of key lawyers currently serving the client, which the designated interviewer(s) will also attend. At this meeting, the group will review all information gathered to date and discuss any service problems, concerns, current issues and potential opportunities. This discussion will help to shape the thrust of the interview by establishing objectives and key priorities.

6. Contact client and set up interview

The client relationship partner should email and call the client to alert them to the request for an interview and explain why the firm is conducting the process. The client should be given a preference for where, when and how to meet. In most cases, clients prefer to keep an interview to 30 or 40 minutes. In some cases, clients may choose to meet for a longer time period, but this should be left up to the client and the interviewer should build flexibility into the schedule to allow for the interview to run over.

Even with the most loyal clients and the best of intentions, clients will cancel or stand you up for pre-scheduled interviews. This is why some prefer the phone to in-person, so that they won't inconvenience you if they have to reschedule. Often, the most effective approach is to find out when they have down time in the office (eg, 7:30 am or 6:30 pm), and try to catch them at that time. Secretaries and executive assistants can be your best allies in scheduling and ensuring follow-through to interview commitments.

Cautionary note: *Some partners try to make the process more informal by meeting over lunch or dinner. However, the interview itself should be conducted as a formal meeting, which can then be followed by a social meal.*

7. Conducting the interview

The interview will have several components to it and will usually include the following.

7.1 Introduction

Depending on who has been selected, the interviewer(s) may be introducing themselves to the client for the first time. Start off the interview with some small talk and rapport building. Remind them why the firm is undertaking the process, what your role is and how the information will be used to their benefit. Tell them that you will be taking notes and offer them a copy of your interview questions to follow during the interview. Encourage candour and discuss how sensitive or confidential information will be handled. Ask them to tell you during the interview if they would prefer to keep any information confidential; but discourage this, as all input is critical to a successful relationship. Remind them that the interview is only scheduled to take half an hour to an hour, and to let you know if a conflict arises.

7.2 Assessment/audit

Using the interview form as a guideline, begin the interview questions. Let clients talk for as long as they wish, but try to bring the interview back into focus so that you can cover the key areas outlined in the form. Let the client take the lead, but probe if you feel that there is more information you need or if you sense a problem, hesitation or ambivalence. You should take notes during the interview.

7.3 Fielding complaints

During the interview, you may hear some candid criticism. Remain as neutral as possible and be certain that you understand the basis and details of the problem from the client's perspective. Be prepared to respond to some of these questions or criticisms, and ask the client how they would like you to handle the problem. Encourage the client to allow you to bring this information back to the individual or team in a constructive way. Promise (and deliver) follow-up.

7.4 Closing the interview

As you near the end of certain sections or the interview itself, remember to ask clients whether they have questions or anything more to add. Brief the client about what will happen next and thank them for their time and input.

8. Post-meeting follow-up and debriefing

In order for clients to feel that the feedback process has been a success, the follow-up to the interview and ongoing implementation of enhancements will be critical. Within 24 hours of conducting the interview, both the relationship partner (who has been informed by the interviewer) and the interviewer should send an email of thanks to the client contact(s) for their time and their insights. In addition, the following steps should be taken.

8.1 Report summary

Within one week of returning from the client, the interviewer should draft a summary of the interview assessment along with recommendations for follow-up steps Particularly sensitive issues or immediate concerns should be addressed immediately with the client relationship partner and/or the managing partner.

8.2 Internal review meeting

Within two weeks of the interview, the managing partner should meet with each client relationship partner to share the typed interview summary and discuss specific follow-up steps. If a marketing/client relations director is involved and present, they should take notes of follow-up action steps and offer to draft a short action plan. Alternatively, the consultant may be asked to do this.

8.3 Review input and suggestions with client

The client relationship partner should review the input and suggested action steps and, within four weeks of the interview, schedule a call or meeting with the client to review specific steps that are recommended to improve service practices, address concerns or pursue opportunities and ways to add value. In rare instances, the client may be unhappy with whomever the key relationship partner is. Whether the client insists upon a change or not, the managing partner and/or department chair should discuss this and carefully consider changing the relationship or matter-specific partner to someone else. Ideally, the client during the interview will have expressed a preference for another partner that they are working with.

8.4 Client team debriefing

The client relationship partner, along with the interviewer and the marketing/client relations director, should lead a meeting to review the findings of the interview. All members of the client service team should attend the meeting; staff may be included or can be convened for a second meeting. At this meeting, the initial draft of an action plan should be reviewed and additional strategies proposed to respond to issues raised in the interview. In addition to the current service team, others may be added to the list for consultation (eg, billing administrator, information systems manager, personnel administrator).

8.5 Follow-up action plan

Following the team meeting, an action plan will be finalised to implement all action items required by the client or raised by the client service team, to address problems; improve services; cross-sell; or follow up on particular client trends, business needs or opportunities. The action plan should specify who is responsible and a completion date for each item, and should be reviewed monthly or bi-monthly by the managing partner and/or the client relations/marketing director.

Appendix IV. Sample client relationship and feedback questions

1. State of the client's business

- How are you doing?
  [Note: Make reference here to any specific milestones or challenges that the company has been facing.] How did the year conclude for the company or what kind of a year has it been so far? Do you anticipate any surprises in the first/second/third/fourth quarter?
- What strategic business changes have you made in the last 12 months?
- What has been particularly difficult or challenging for your business in the last 12 months?
- How and where do you see things heading next year for the business and the industry, and what are the greatest challenges you face?
- What are the top goals and priorities for the business over the next 12 months? What might impede or prevent the company from achieving its goals?
- What new products or services do you anticipate launching in the next year or two?
- What are your plans for market expansion? In which countries?
- Will you be closing facilities?
- How would you describe the culture of the company?

2. The legal department, your role and future needs/approaches

- Has your role changed in the past year and if so, how? What are your primary responsibilities?
- What is your greatest personal challenge in your role?
- What are your current hiring needs in the legal department? How can we help you with this? Can we help send candidates your way?
- How is the legal department currently structured? Any recent changes? How many lawyers? Other professionals?
- How does the legal department serve the needs of the business? Are you segmented by practice area/skillset/business unit? How does the legal team interact with the functional areas that affect compliance and legal (eg, HR, IT, privacy, compliance, marketing and sales, contracting, outsourcing, sponsorships, finance)?
- Where do you see your legal needs changing in the coming year? Any new needs or challenges?
- Approximately how much do you spend on outside legal services annually?
- What are your top legal, risk and compliance priorities for the next 12 months?
- What are your greatest needs for legal services now? How are

you managing these – for example, which of these are you asking your own legal team to perform and which are you sending to outside law firms?
- Are you using other service providers for any legal needs (eg, ALSPs, LPOs, e-discovery vendors)? How is that working for you?
- What have you automated with technology/AI?
- What do you most value in your outside lawyers, law firms or law companies?
- Do you prefer to work with a large number of firms or a smaller number?
- Are there any lawyers or firms that you look to as 'go-to' counsel? If so, who are they, what areas do you use them for and what qualities make them 'go-to' counsel?
- Do you plan any changes in the ways you work with outside counsel?
- Are you planning to go through an RFP process or convergence process in the coming year? How will that work?

3. Overall feedback on firm's performance
- How would you rate your overall satisfaction with the work that our firm has performed?
- How well do you like working with our firm? What could we do to improve that experience for you?
- How well have we done managing our relationship with you?
- How would you describe the quality of the work product and the results that we have produced for you?
- How well did we listen to your concerns and understand your goals?
- How effectively do we communicate with you and keep you informed?
- How well do you think our internal teams coordinate your various matters for you?
- How could we become better aligned with and interact with your internal team?
- Have the firm's fees and costs been reasonable for the service provided?
- With which attorneys in our firm do you have direct or some contact? How would you describe the performance of each attorney? Do you have specific observations to share about individual lawyers (either those who exceeded your expectations or those who were less effective)?
- Are we staffing your matters the way you would like us to and are we efficient?
- Are our fees fair and reasonable? How do these compare with others?
- With which attorneys in our firm do you have direct contact or

some contact? How would you describe the performance of each attorney?
- How does the service you currently receive from us compare to that of other firms or attorneys you have worked with in the past or present?
- What distinguishes our firm from other law firms?
- If you do not use us for all of your legal needs, is there anything that limits our ability to fully serve your legal needs?

4. Specific feedback on the firm's performance

1. On a scale of 0-10 – where 0 is "Does not happen at all" and 10 is "Exceptional/consistently exceeds expectations", please share with us how we are doing in the following areas.

Responsiveness and communication
- Available and accessible?
- Consistently deliver work when or before you need it?
- Return phone calls as promptly as you wish?
- Keep you informed on the status of cases, matters or transactions as often as you would like?
- Discuss matters with you in a succinct and user-friendly manner?
- Proactively reach out to you with issues or trends we see that might affect you or the business?

Work product
- Have in-depth knowledge of the legal issues?
- Give you thoughtful, well-reasoned advice?
- Quickly focus on and resolve key issues?
- Solve problems creatively and innovatively?
- Consistently maintain error-free, high quality?
- Understand your business and the issues that impact on the organisation?
- Understand how your business operates as a commercial enterprise?
- Understand your industry?
- Deliver work consistently across practice groups and offices?

Attitude
- Work well with everyone in your organisation?
- Enthusiastic about helping you achieve your goal?
- Courteous as attorneys?
- Courteous as staff?

Project management, cost and efficiency
- Staff projects effectively and efficiently, putting the right people on the matter?

- Eliminate 'surprises' by seeking advance approval?
- Propose and implement cost-effective solutions?
- Discuss and propose alternative fees and pricing?
- Understand the relationship of legal strategies to your business goals?
- Keep you informed of status of cases and strategies as often as you wish?
- Accurately estimate the cost of service and project scope?
- Respond to your billing inquiries promptly?
- Send bills that are timely, accurate and easy to understand?

Intangibles

- Treat you as an important client?
- Add value to our relationship beyond what is required?
- Keep you informed on new legal trends and issues?
- Serve as a strategic sounding board and trusted adviser for you?
- Make you feel comfortable dealing with others when your primary contact isn't there?

2. In what ways have we performed very well for you or exceeded your expectations? Please describe a time when we exceeded your expectations.

3. In which specific areas have we disappointed you or do we need to improve? Please share specifics with us. Please describe a situation when you were very disappointed and feel that you should have received better service.

5. How we could improve our value and effectiveness

- Please share with us your views on:
  - the greatest value we deliver;
  - how we can provide better value and help you to contain your legal costs;
  - whether you use alternative billing arrangements with other firms that you would like us to consider;
  - whether there is any work you would not send to us because of cost factors; and
  - how else we could add value to you/our relationship.
- Of the value-add efforts we are making on your behalf, what do you find helpful and what are not all that helpful (eg, webinars, client alerts, secondments, on-site CLEs, 'around the corner' briefings, access to our knowledge bank)?
- Are there things that you wish all law firms would do differently or practices they would adopt?
- Are there specific ways in which other firms are better serving you than we are? Different approaches, tools, technologies, staffing models we might learn from? Is there anything else you

can share with us that would help us better meet your needs next year? What more can we do to better serve you? Add value to you personally? To your legal department? To other areas of the business? What can we do to help you be successful?

- If you do not use us for all of your legal needs, is there anything that limits our ability to fully serve those needs for you?
- Would you recommend our firm to others? Have you had a chance to do so?
- Is there any other advice you can share with us?

Appendix V. American Bar Association Resolution 113 to help promote diversity in the legal profession survey

As stated previously,[36] there have been a number of efforts by general counsel and chief legal officers to define expectations and metrics for their law firms on their D&I efforts in a bid to promote sustainable diversity in the profession. In 2016, the American Bar Association (ABA) enacted Resolution 113 to help clients hold their law firms accountable. Corporate clients are encouraged to ask their outside law firms to complete the Model Diversity Survey in order to procure and evaluate legal service providers.

For general information about Resolution 113 and the Model Diversity Survey, visit www.americanbar.org/groups/diversity/Diversity Commission/model-diversity-survey/.

For background to Resolution 113 and its signatories, visit www.americanbar.org/content/dam/aba/administrative/racial_ethnic_diversity/aba/letter_from_the_signatories_general_counsel_implementation_of_aba_resolution_113.pdf.

Appendix VI. Case study: Kristen Cook, associate general counsel, 7-Eleven, Inc and SEI Fuel Services, Inc; and winner of two ACC Value Champion Awards

1. 7-Eleven/Seyfarth Shaw Value Champion project

- Need:
  - A real estate portfolio of 10,000-plus properties in the United States and Canada grew by 10% after a 2018 acquisition. This was too heavy a load for two in-house real estate lawyers to handle, so they were using a lot of outside lawyer help.
- Components of the redesigned service model:
  - Value-based, hybrid insourcing and outsourcing staffing realignment workflow.
  - Dedicated 7-Eleven website to streamline communications among the legal team and 100 real estate professionals – daily deal tracking and budget tracking in real time.
  - Detailed, 15-page process map that identified inefficient steps.
  - Consistency in processes for negotiation and lease provisions.
  - A series of flat and alternative fees to assist with predictable budgeting and reduced cost.
- Outcomes:
  - In the first eight months, reduced outside counsel spend by 19%.
  - New store deal fall-through rates decreased from 25% to 1%.
  - 80% of all real estate disputes now handled in-house.

2. 7-Eleven/Perkins Coie Value Champion project

- Need:
  - Due to exponential growth of merchandise sales through stores and digitally, needed to manage substantial volumes of work through outsourcing and inside lawyer involvement.
- Components:
  - Dynamic intake forms.
  - Automated notifications activating legal processes and assigning matters to Perkins Coie legal team.
  - Shared document repository.
  - Tools that provide customised and real-time visualisation, status tracking and reporting.
  - Dedicated legal project manager and on-site contract manager.
- Outcomes:
  - Reduced time spent opening matters, locating matter-related documents, assessing the status and quantifying portfolio metrics.
  - Weekly and quarterly metrics provided through portal.

- Mature procurement model replacing prior email process; now 84%+ of all new digital/IT and merchandising matters originate through portal.
- Fixed monthly fee, predictable budgeting.
- Inclusion of non-traditional professionals (eg, knowledge management and project managers).
- Since 2018, reduced per matter cost by 18% for digital/IT contracts and 66% for merchandising contracts.

Notes

1 Frederick F Reichheld and W Earl Sasser, Jr, "Zero Defections: Quality Comes to Service", *Harvard Business Review*, September-October 1990.
2 James L Heskett, W Earl Sasser, Jr and Leonard A Schlesinger, "The Service Profit Chain", *Free Press*, 10 April 1997.
3 Reichheld and Sasser, Jr (n 1).
4 Frederick F Reichheld, *Loyalty Rules: How Today's Leaders Build Lasting Relationships* (Harvard Business Review Press, 2003).
5 In 2020, several US states began to modify or eliminate the American Bar Association's Model Rule of Professional Conduct Rule 5.4, Professional Independence of a Lawyer. This includes several provisions: "A lawyer or law firm shall not share legal fees with a nonlawyer"; a "lawyer shall not form a partnership with a nonlawyer"; and a lawyer shall not practise law for profit if "a nonlawyer owns any interest therein"; and "[l]egal services must be provided by a law firm that is owned, managed, and financed exclusively by lawyers". By eliminating or modifying Rule 5.4, non-lawyers may be able to share ownership in a law firm in those states.
6 With appreciation and acknowledgement of contributions to some portions of this chapter by Jonathan Hollenberg of HawkPartners LLC.
7 The single question is: "On a scale of 0–10, how likely is it that you would recommend [name of law firm] to a colleague?"
8 www.legalbusinessworld.com/post/the-shape-of-lawyers-in-the-future-t-o-or-delta.
9 *Ibid.*
10 *Dale Carnegie, How to Win Friends and Influence People* (Simon & Schuster, 2011).
11 www.entrepreneur.com/article/239831.
12 https://salesbenchmarkindex.com/insights/key-account-management-avoiding-the-bow-tie-resource-approach/.
13 Inconsistency in service and quality is often something that clients complain about when working with multiple offices and lawyers in large national and international firms.
14 www.diversitylab.com/mansfield-rule-4-0/.
15 www.acc.com/resource-library/unless-you-ask-guide-law-departments-get-more-external-relationships.
16 The American Society for Quality states: "Lean Six Sigma is a fact-based, data-driven philosophy of improvement that values defect prevention over defect detection. It drives customer satisfaction and bottom-line results by reducing variation, waste, and cycle time, while promoting the use of work standardization and flow, thereby creating a competitive advantage. It applies anywhere variation and waste exist, and every employee should be involved." See www.greycampus.com/blog/quality-management/a-brief-introduction-to-lean-and-six-sigma-and-lean-six-sigma.
17 More information about PERSUIT can be found at www.persuit.com.
18 Heidi K Gardner, *Smart Collaboration: How Professionals and Their Firms Succeed in Breaking Down Silos* (Harvard Business Review Press, 2016).
19 Dr Larry Richard is recognised as the leading expert on the psychology of lawyer behaviour. A graduate of the University of Pennsylvania Law School, Dr Richard practised law as a trial attorney for 10 years before earning a PhD in psychology from Temple University. He is the founder of the legal management consulting firm LawyerBrain.
20 Dr Heidi K Gardner is a distinguished fellow at Harvard Law School's Center on the Legal Profession and Faculty Chair of Harvard Law School's Accelerated Leadership Program and Smart Collaboration Masterclass. She has published many books and articles on collaboration and leadership, and launched Smart Collaboration Accelerator™ – a tool that helps team leaders and individuals to assess their collaboration behavioural preferences to help enhance effective teams, integrate laterals and better serve clients.
21 www.mcca.com/call-action-sara-lees-general-counsel-making-diversity-priority/.
22 www.americanbar.org/groups/diversity/DiversityCommission/model-diversity-survey/.
23 Reported in *American Lawyer* by Christine Simmons, 27 January 2019.
24 https://newsroom.intel.com/editorials/intel-rule-action-improve-diversity-legal-profession/#gs.ooopqy.
25 www.reuters.com/article/lawyer-diversity-microsoft/microsoft-raises-reward-for-outside-law-firms-that-promote-black-and-latino-lawyers-idUSL1N2GR1LH.
26 www.payscale.com/compensation-today/2019/03/tie-bonuses-to-diversity-goals.
27 www.law.com/sites/almstaff/2017/05/30/meet-the-gcs-who-may-finally-move-the-needle-on-diversity/?slreturn=20201129101112.
28 www.legalmosaic.com/corporate-departments-are-taking-the-lead-in-creating-a-more-diverse-legal-industry/.
29 www.diversitylab.com/knowledge-sharing/clients-push-for-diversity/.
30 www.diversitylab.com/knowledge-sharing/clients-push-for-diversity/.
31 www.mcca.com/mcca-article/engage-excellence/.
32 www.diversitylab.com/knowledge-sharing/clients-push-for-diversity/.
33 Authored by and reprinted with permission of Jeff Carr, former senior vice president and general counsel at Univar Solutions and FMC Technologies.
34 Authored by and reprinted with permission of Jeff Carr, former senior vice president and general counsel at Univar Solutions and FMC Technologies.
35 See Part 3, Chapter IV for a full discussion on client feedback programmes.
36 See Part 5, Chapter VI.